1783 TAX LIST of BALTIMORE COUNTY MARYLAND

Abstracted by
Robert W. Barnes
and
Bettie Stirling Carothers

Maps by
George J. Horvath, Jr.

HERITAGE BOOKS
2010

HERITAGE BOOKS
AN IMPRINT OF HERITAGE BOOKS, INC.

Books, CDs, and more—Worldwide

For our listing of thousands of titles see our website at
www.HeritageBooks.com

Published 2010 by
HERITAGE BOOKS, INC.
Publishing Division
100 Railroad Ave. #104
Westminster, Maryland 21157

Originally published in 1978 by Bettie S. Carothers

All rights reserved. No part of this book may be reproduced or transmitted in any form or by any means, electronic or mechanical, including photocopying, recording or by any information storage and retrieval system without written permission from the author, except for the inclusion of brief quotations in a review.

International Standard Book Numbers
Paperbound: 978-1-58549-364-7
Clothbound: 978-0-7884-8495-7

CONTENTS

Preface iii
The Hundreds of Baltimore County iv

Maps:

Key to the 1783 Hundred vi
Patapsco Upper Hundred vii
Soldiers Delight Hundred viii
Back River Lower Hundred ix
Delaware Hundred After 1755 x
Baltimore East Hundred - called Old Town xi
Gunpowder Upper Hundred xii
Middle River Lower Hundred xiii
Middlesex Hundred xiv
Part of Deptford Hundred xv
Middle River Upper Hundred and Back River Upper Hundred .. xvi
Mine Run Hundred xvii
North Hundred xviii
Patapsco Lower Hundred xix
Pipe Creek Hundred xx

1783 Tax lists:

Back River Lower Hundred 1
Baltimore East Hundred - called Old Town 8
Delaware Upper Hundred 13
Deptford Hundred 21
Gunpowder Upper Hundred 27
Middle River Lower Hundred 37
Middlesex Hundred 44
Middle River Upper Hundred and Back River Upper Hundred ... 49
Mine Run Hundred 63
North Hundred 71
Patapsco Lower Hundred 82
Pipe Creek Hundred 88

Index to the Tract Names 98
Index to the Surnames 108

PREFACE

In early Maryland the church parishes were used as georgaphical divisions and from this, parishes were divided into hundreds. The term hundreds steming from the English, who early used this division to mean land which supported a hundred families or could raise a hundred soldiers. It was in this way that the tax assessor was appointed and the taxes raised.

The "1783 Tax List of Baltimore County, Maryland", can be found in the Scharf collection at the Maryland Historical Society, where it can also be seen on microfilm. Arranged by hundreds showing the names of the land owners, the tract names, the number of acres in each tract, the paupers (denoted by (P) and included anyone who owned less than ten pounds in property). Bachelors are noted with those who were their securities and who were many times closely related to the bachelors. The number of inhabitants are listed; but the information given varied with the tax assessor. It must be assumed that where the number of inhabitants is not given, that although the person listed did in fact own the land, he resided elsewhere.

We do feel it necessary to advise anyone using this material to check every possible spelling for both surnames and land names. Two errors made by the assessor have been brought to our attention by a knowledgeable friend, Mr. George J. Horvath, Jr. Mr. Horvath states "Mt. Hase" should read as "Mt. Hays" and on page 2, "Sophias Garden Resurveyed" owned by the Fitch family, should be listed as "Fitches Chance" and was never called "Sophias Garden Resurveyed" although the assessor lists it this way.

A special thanks is given to Mr. Robert W. Barnes who graciously contributed the abstracts of the majority of the hundreds. Mr. Barnes, a well known and respected Maryland genealogist has been a driving force in seeing this Baltimore County source published.

Without the knowledge and talent of Mr. George J. Horvath, it would not have been possible to include the maps of the hundreds that make this volume so much more valuable. Many hours of research and work went into the finalizing of the maps and we are deeply indebted to George Horvath for them.

Mrs. Margaret Cameron added her special help and expertise in the area of Mine Run and North Hundreds and we owe her a large debt of gratitude. It is my hope that we have helped genealogists and historians, present and future, with this addition to Maryland source books now in print.

The Hundreds of Baltimore County

by Robert Barnes

BACK RIVER LOWER HUNDRED was in existence at least by 1773 when its inhabitants were included in a tax list of the county.

BACK RIVER UPPER HUNDRED was created by 1731 when Thomas Ford was appointed constable of the hundred. It was adjacent to Soldiers Delight Hundred for in 1742 the two hundreds were included in the then newly created St. Thomas Parish.
    The Southern boundary of this hundred was the Old Court Road that led from Patapsco Falls to Joppa. On the East line was the dividing line between St. Pauls (later St. Thomas) Parish and St. Johns Parish(i.e., Big Gunpowder Falls, Western Run, and Piney Run). The Western boundary, between Back River Upper and Soldiers Delight Hundred was probably Herring Run or Jones Falls, and the Northern boundary was no doubt Maryland Line.

BALTIMORE TOWN EAST HUNDRED and BALTIMORE TOWN WEST HUNDRED were both in existence by 1773 when their inhabitants were included in the tax list for the county.

DELAWARE HUNDRED, lying in the forks of the Patapsco, was created in 1755 out of a part of Soldiers Delight Hundred. In the 1783 tax list the hundred was called Delaware Upper Hundred.
    The hundred began where the Old Indian Road crossed the main falls of Patapsco (where James Dawkins lived), and was bounded on the North by the said Indian Road until it intersected the Frederick County Line.

DEPTFORD HUNDRED was in existence by 1773 when it's inhabitants were included in the tax list of the county.

GUNPOWDER UPPER HUNDRED may have originally been called North Side of Gunpowder Hundred, but was definitely known as Gunpowder Upper Hundred after 1741. After c.1758 the hundred was called Mine Run Hundred, or else Mine Run Hundred was created out of part of the hundred. Gunpowder Upper and Mine Run Hundreds were both in existence by 1774.

MIDDLE RIVER LOWER HUNDRED was in existence by 1773 when it's inhabitants were included in a tax list.

MIDDLE RIVER UPPER HUNDRED was included in a 1705 tax list of the county. At that time it may have been another name for North Side of Back River Hundred.
    When St. James Parish was created in 1770 the Act of Assembly stated that the parish was to include that part of Middle River Upper Hundred lying North of the road that leads from the main road from Baltimore to York, where (the side road) it crosses the South branch of Gunpowder at Walter Dulany's plantation.

MIDDLESEX HUNDRED was in existence by 1774 when it was included in a list of the hundreds.

MINE RUN HUNDRED was created c.1758 out of a part of Gunpowder Upper Hundred.
    The Act of 1770 which established St. James Parish stated that Mine Run Hundred was to be included in the parish.

NORTH HUNDRED was in existence by 1770 when it is mentioned in the Act of Assembly as being included in St. James Parish.

PATAPSCO LOWER HUNDRED was in existence by 1773 when it was included in the tax list of the county.

PATAPSCO UPPER HUNDRED was in existence at least as early as 1730 when William Hammond was appointed road overseer for that part of Upper Patapsco lying between the rolling road from Soldiers's Delight (to) Gwynns Falls to the landing, all between the main road leading from Patapsco Falls inclusive of both roads.
    In November 1733 the county court ordered that this hundred be divided along the Court Road (now Old Court Road) until it intersected Gardiner's Glade and then ran with the said glade to the main falls of the Patapsco. The North side of the Hundred was to be called Soldier's Delight Hundred.

PIPE CREEK HUNDRED was created out of Soldier's Delight Hundred in 1755. It contained all that part of Baltimore County North of the Indian Road that led from the Great Falls of Patapsco to where James Dawkins lived until it intersected Frederick County, that was not in Middle River or Back River Hundreds.
    Mr. Marye places the line between Soldiers Delight and Pipe Creek Hundred as running Southeast from Westminster between Beaver Dam Run and Patapsco Falls until the line crossed the latter slightly above the junction of Roaring Run and the Falls.

SOLDIERS DELIGHT HUNDRED was created out of Patapsco Upper Hundred in 1733.
    In November 1755 the Baltimore County Court ordered Soldiers Delight Hundred to be divided into three hundreds: Delaware, Pipe Creek and Soldiers Delight Hundred.
    The Tax List for this hundred in 1783 has not been preserved.

WESTMINSTER HUNDRED was in existence by 1733 when it was included in the tax list of the county.

                      Selected References
1- Baltimore County Court Proceedings, Hall of Records.
2- Marye, William B., "The Old Indian Road," <u>Md. His. Mag.</u>, XV (1920, 107 ff.
3- Scharf, John Thomas, <u>History of Baltimore City & County</u>, Baltimore: Regional Pub. Co., 1971
4- Spencer, Edward, "Soldier's Delight Hundred," Md. His. Mag., I(1906), 141 ff.
5- Wilkins, Wm. N., Baltimore County Tax List for 1773, typescript at Md. His. Soc.

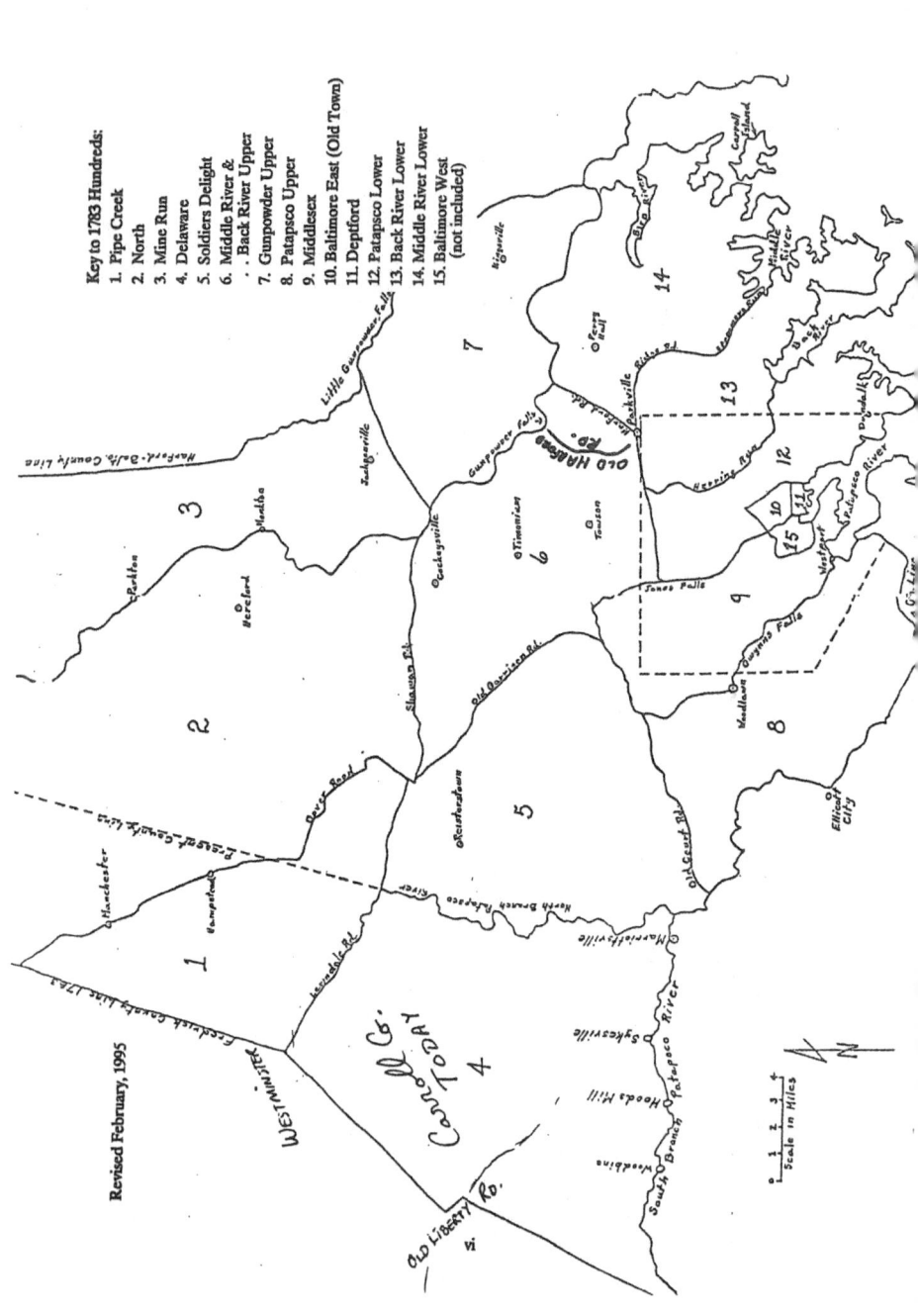

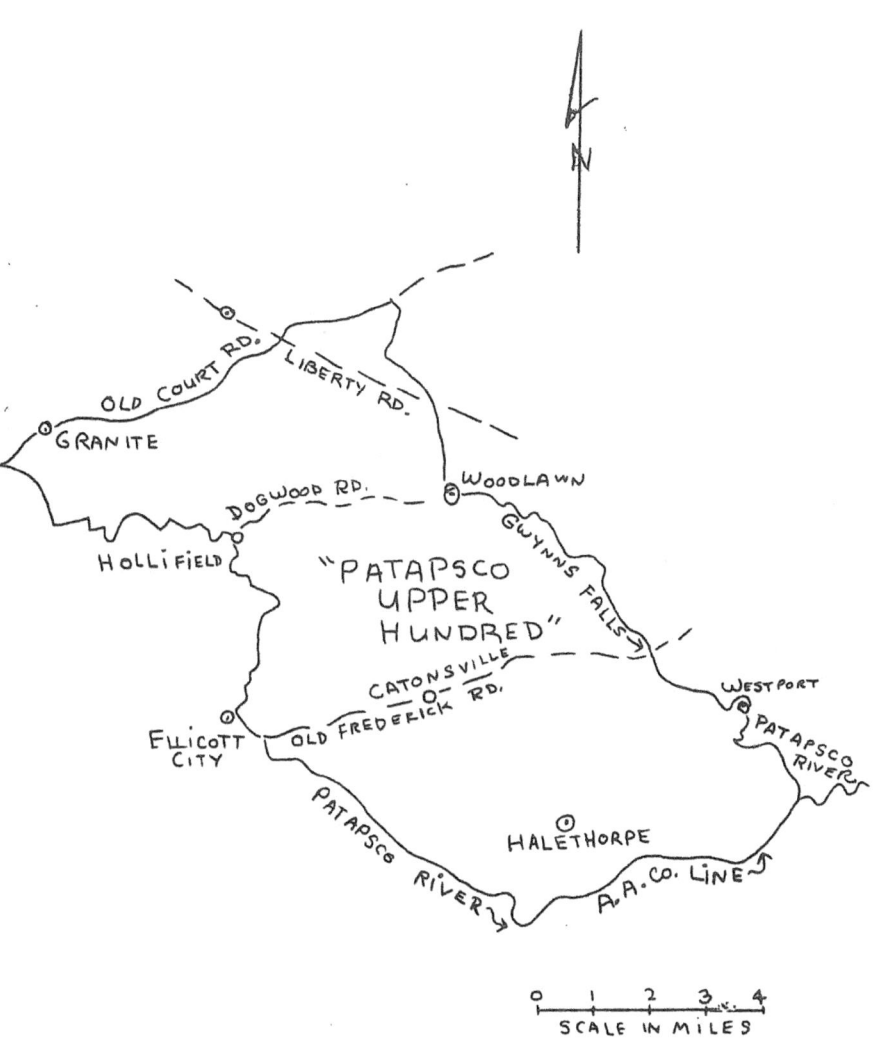

As assumed by
George J. Horvath, Jr.
February 1978

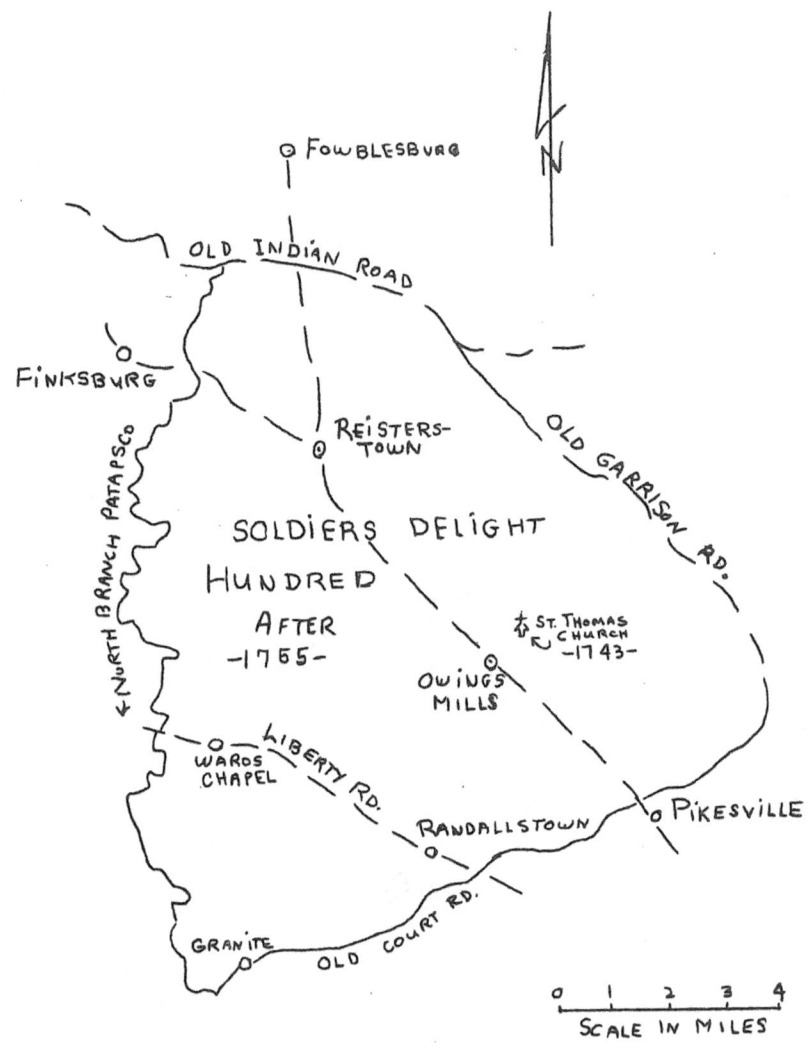

As assumed by
George J. Horvath, Jr.
February 1978

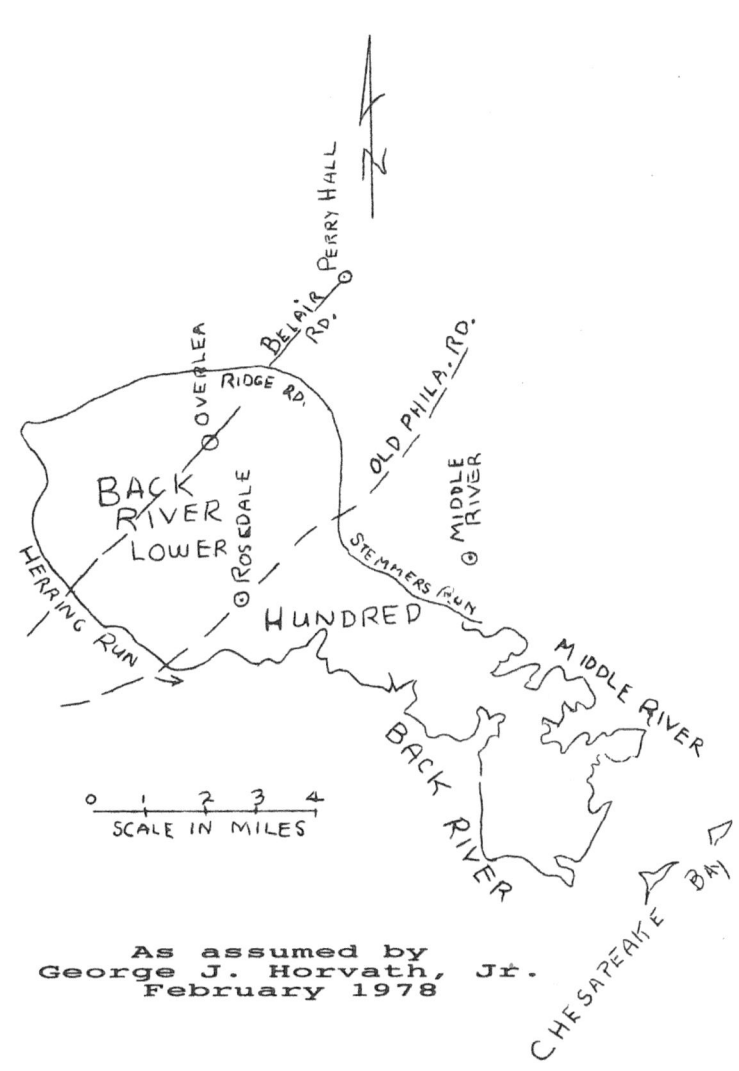

As assumed by
George J. Horvath, Jr.
February 1978

As assumed by
George J. Horvath, Jr.
February 1978

SCALE IN MILES
0 1 2 3 4

N

COUNTY LINE IN 1783
COUNTY LINE

"DELAWARE HUNDRED" AFTER 1755

FREDERICK
BALTIMORE

WESTMINSTER
FINKSBURG
LAWNDALE RD.
WESTMINSTER PIKE
ROAD TO JOPPA
DEER PARK ROAD
WINFIELD
OLD LIBERTY Rd.
OLD DISCRETE RD / WHISKEY Rd
HOLY TRINITY CHURCH 1771
ELDERSBURG
LIBERTY
MARRIOTTSVILLE

WOODBINE
HOODS MILL
SYKESVILLE
PATAPSCO RIVER
BRANCH
South

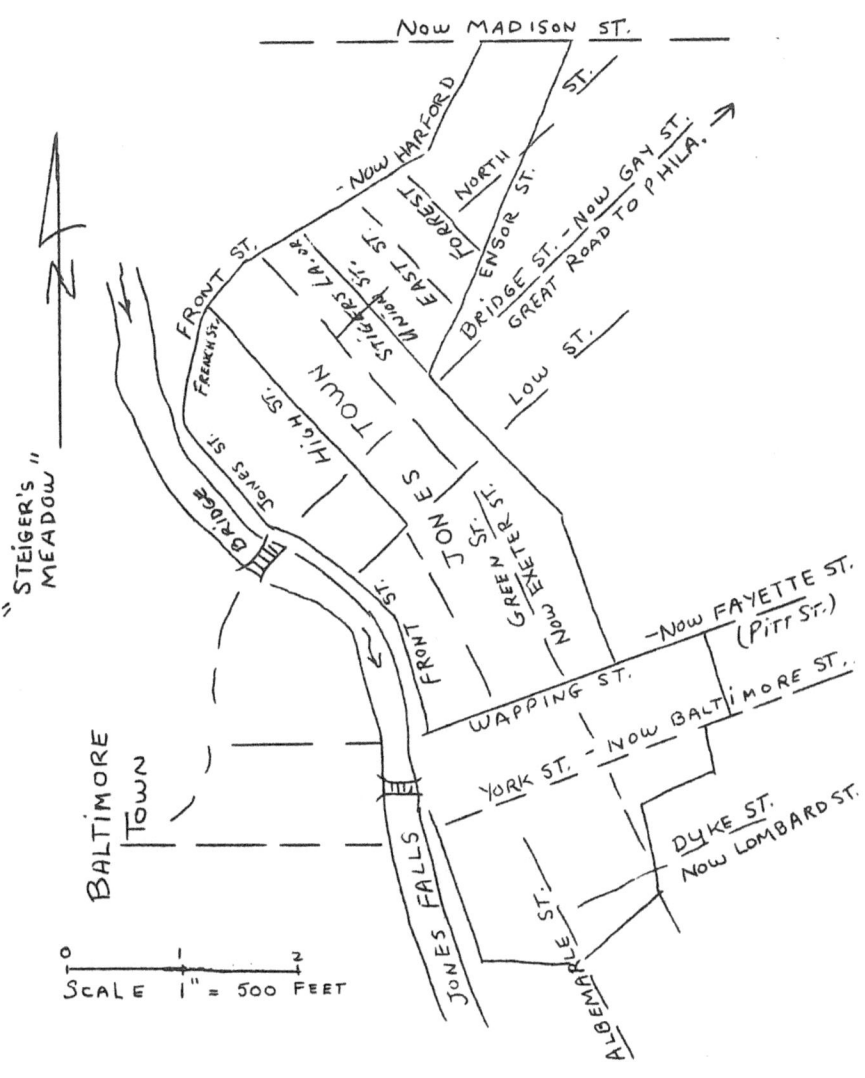

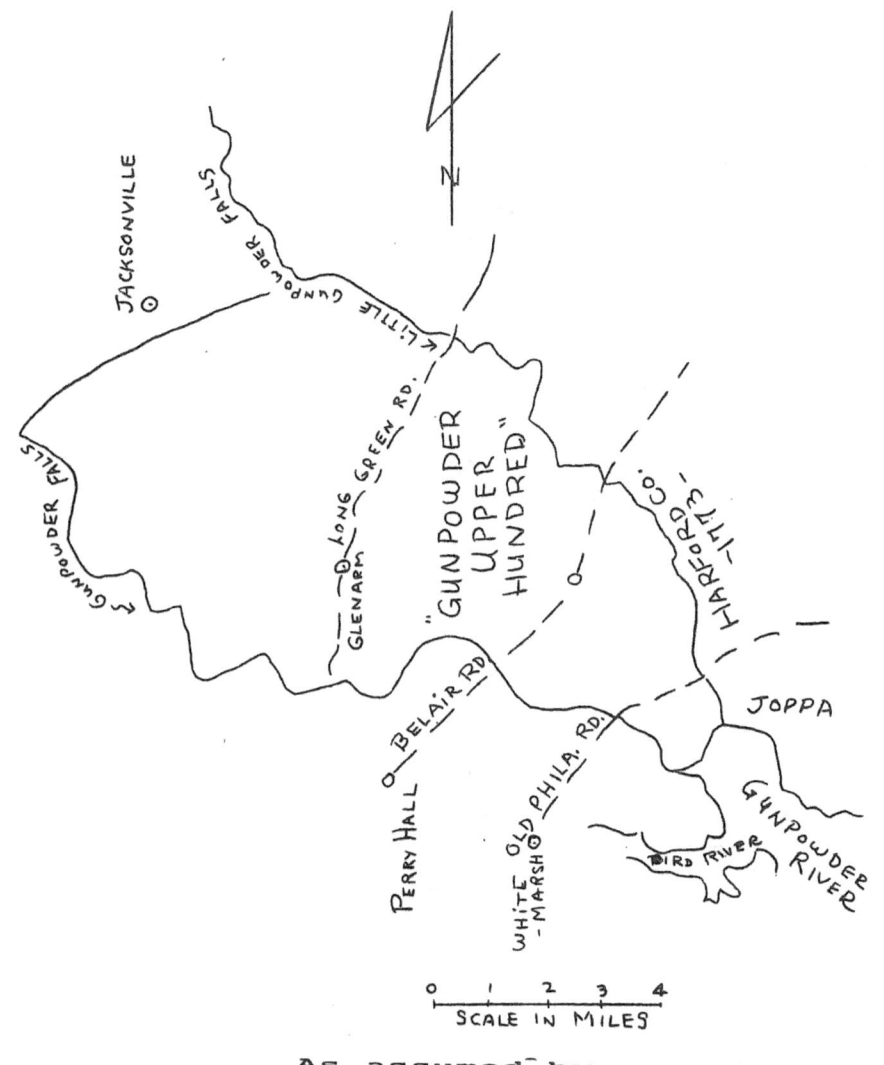

As assumed by
George J. Horvath, Jr.
February 1978

As assumed by George J. Horvath, Jr.
February, 1978. Revised February, 1995

As assumed by
George J. Horvath, Jr.
February 1978

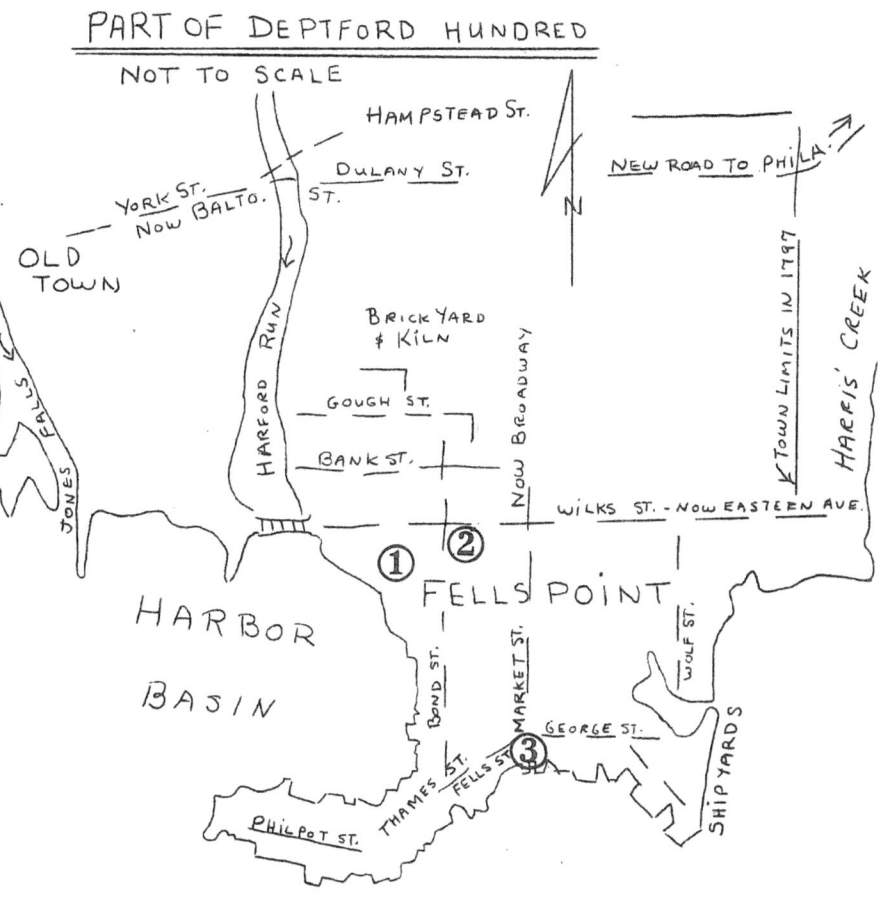

As Assumed by
Shirley Clemens
April 1978

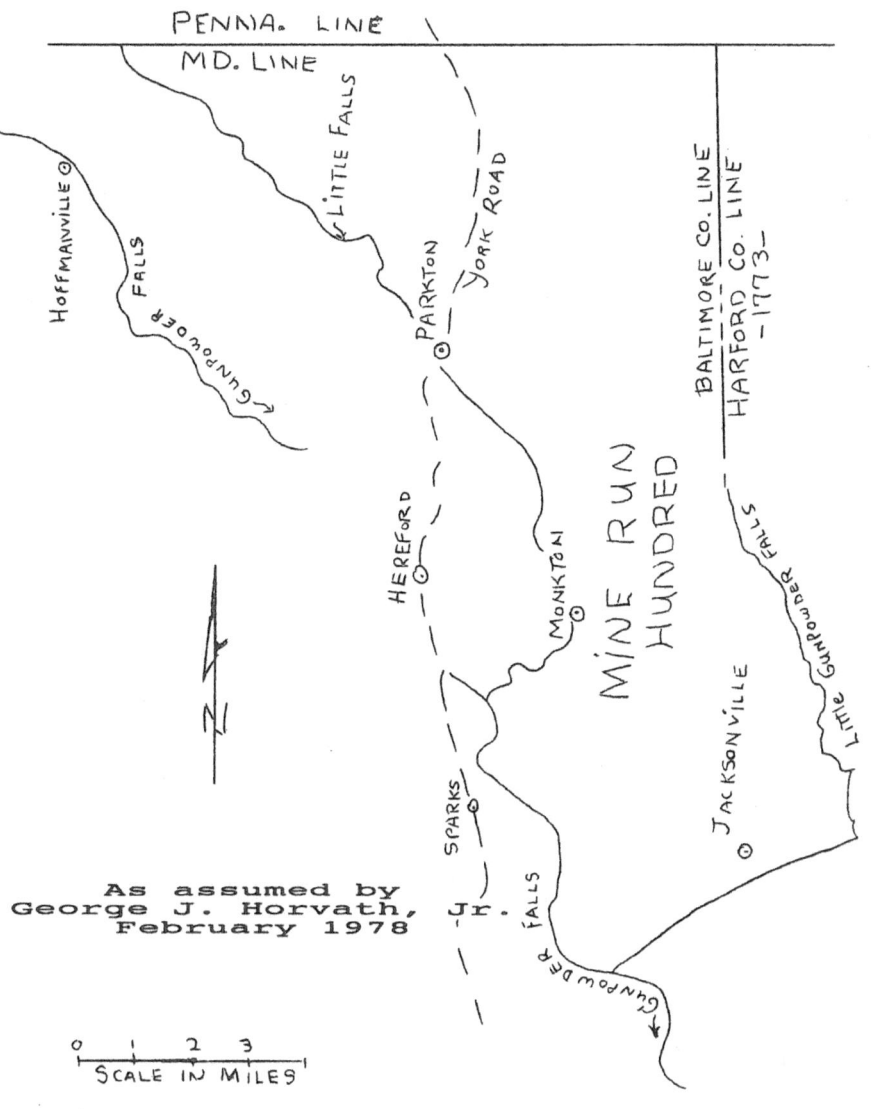

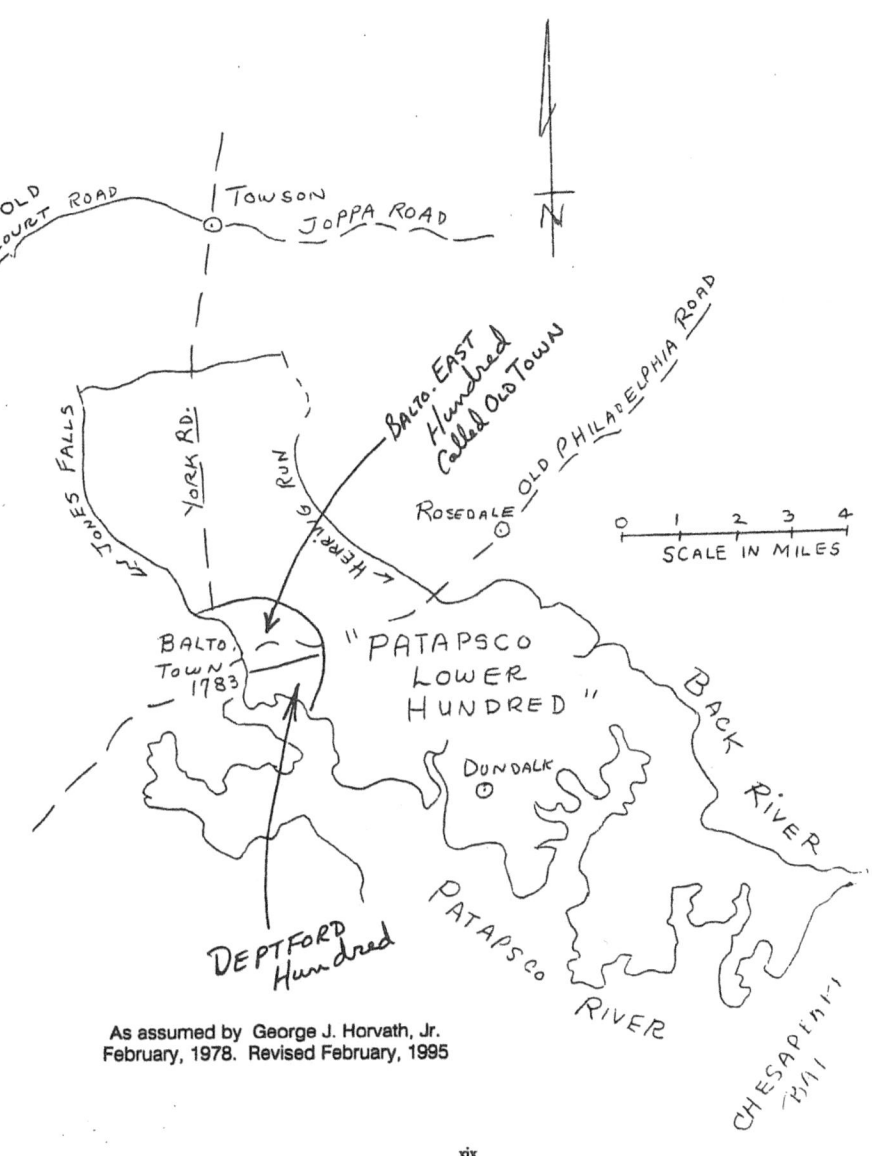

As assumed by George J. Horvath, Jr.
February, 1978. Revised February, 1995

1783 TAX LIST OF BALTIMORE COUNTY, MARYLAND
Back River Lower Hundred

The 1783 Tax List, found in the Scharf collection at the Maryland Historical Society, show that there were 21,597 2/3 acres of land. The list contains 471 free males, including 29 bachelors and 57 paupers and 948 white inhabitants

Owners	Tract Name	# Acres	Free Males	Total White Inhabitants
Armstrong, James			3	7
Asher, John			2	6
Barton, Greenbury	Daniels Plains	100	4	6
Barton, John			4	6
Baylis Jonas	pt. Sophiers Garden Regulated-132		3	5
Bidderson, Daniel	pt. Biddersons Neck	200	2	3
Bidderson, Jeremiah	pt. Biddersons Neck	166	1	1
Bidderson, Shadrack	pt. Harbour	50	2	3
Bidderson, Thomas Sr.	pt. The Harbour	70		
	pt. Small Valley Near	12	4	7
Bidderson, Thomas Jr.	pt. Add. to Harbour	50	4	6
Diddle, Jesse	pt. Egypt	1	1	5
Bivens, Jesse			3	6
Bond, Buckler	pt. Paradise Regained	443		
Bond Thomas of John	pt. Stansburys Inheritance	445		
Bond, William			2	4
Boswell Alexander			3	5
Boswell James			3	5
Brown, Dixon	Longworth	123	2	4
Buchanan, Arthur			2	4
Buck, Benjamin, assessor-pt. Fields Forest		100		
	Bachelors Delight	50		
	pt. Harrimans Desire	40		
	surplus land	60	5	8
Buck, James	Outlet to Bushey Neck	170	4	7
Burgin, Thomas	pt. surplus land	20		
	Dear Bit	125		
	Srusbury	65	6	10
Carback, John	Mollys Garden	50	3	5
Carback, Thomas			3	6
Carback, Valentine			4	7
Carter, Jno.	pt. Egypt		1	1
Carter, Joseph	pt. Stoney Hills	20 1/2	1	3
Carter Richard			1	2
Carter, Solomon			1	2
Chase Jeremiah T.	Borings Landing	100		
Christopher, Jno.	Reisters Study	50	6	3

1783 TAX LIST OF BALTIMORE COUNTY, MARYLAND
Back River Lower Hundred

Owners	Tract Name	# Acres	Free Males	Total White Inhabitants
Clark, Benjamin			3	6
Clarke, Samuel Sr.	Harrimans Outlet	100		
	Project	100	4	7
Clarke, Samuel Jr.			1	1
Coale, Richard	Coales Discover	330	4	9
Cole, William			2	7
Cottrill, Thomas Sr.			1	3
Cottrill, Jno.			4	6
Cottrill, Thomas Jr.			3	5
Councilman George	Alexanders Range	125	2	6
Cow, Greenbury for William's heirs				
Cowerd, Fielding	Tolers Disappointment	75	2	10
Cox, Mary	Long Point	50		
	Coxes Privilege	146		
Cromwell, Joseph	pt. Franklins Purchase	44		
	Inloes Lone	100		
	Sollers Point	120		
	The Wedge	65		
	pt. Cherry Garden	50	1	5
Cromwell, William	White Oak Swamp	113		
Dallis (Dollis), Walter	pt. Hopewell	189		
	Bushy Neck	200	3	7
Daugherday, Joseph			1	6
Davis, Richard			2	6
Davis Robert	Dukes Discovery	80	7	12
Dew, Thomas			3	7
Downing, Samuel	pt. Sophiers Garden Regulated-130		1	1
Dukes, Christopher	pt. Norwich	50		
	Cherry Garden	50		
	Hab Nab at a Venture	100	1	3
Eaglestone, Abraham	Come by Chance	150		
Fife, William	pt. Africa	95	2	2
Fitch, Robert	pt. Sophias Garden Regulated-20			
	pt. Sophias Garden & Sophias Garden Resurveyed-161 1/2		2	7
Fitch, Thomas	pt. Sophias Garden & Sophias Garden Resurveyed-79		1	3
Fitch, William	pt. Sophias Garden & pt. Sophias Garden Resurveyed-129		3	5
Fitch, William Jr.	pt. Sophias Garden Regulated-138 pt. Sophias Garden Resurveyed-112 1/2		3	7

1783 TAX LIST OF BALTIMORE COUNTY, MARYLAND
Back River Lower Hundred

Owner	Tract Names	# Acres	Free Males	Total White Inhabitants
Floyd, Joseph			1	2
Fowler, Tamer			2	6
Fowler, Zach'y			1	5
Franklin, Charles			3	7
Franklin, James	Holeys Neck	326	2	6
Franklin, Thomas Sr.				
Galloway, Thomas	pt. Littleworth	53		
	Add. to Littleworth	25	2	3
Garrettson, Job	Bucks Range	750		
	The Gift	123		
	pt. Goshen	100		
	pt. Duck Harbor	214		
	pt. Chevy Chase	200		
	Hines Purchase	211		
	pt. Hazard	50	6	12
Garrettson, Saul	pt. Hines Purchase	50	1	1
Garrettson, Shadrack	pt. Duck Harbour	50		
Gatch, Conduce	Sidmons Last	137	1	5
Gatch, Frederick			4	8
Gatch, Nicholas			1	3
Gest, Thomas	High Germany	74		
	Chance	78		
	Fortune	23 1/2		
Gibbons, Thomas	(Pauper)		1	2
Grant, Hugh	(Pauper)		7	12
Graves, John			3	6
Graves, Thomas			3	5
Green, Vincent			2	7
Green, Patrick			1	2
Griffith, Kinsey			1	3
Grigory, Jas.			4	8
Grigory, John	Privilege	50	3	4
Grimes, Jas.	(Pauper)		2	5
Grimes, Nicholas			3	8
Grove, Jacob			4	8
Hale, Jas. (Bachelor)	Security was Roger Hale			
Hale, Jno.			7	10
Hale, Roger			2	4
Harker, Jno.			3	5
Harryman Ann	pt. Richardsons Forest	24	2	5
Harryman, David	(Pauper)		2	3

1783 TAX LIST OF BALTIMORE, COUNTY MARYLAND
Back River Lower Hundred

Owner	Tract Name	# Acres	Free Males	Total White Inhabitants
Harryman George	Shaws Fancy	100		
	Shaws Privilege	80		
	Shaws Delight	96		
Harryman Jno.	pt. Richardsons Forest	77		
	surplus land	30	2	4
Harryman, Joshua	(Bachelor) Security was Moses Thompson			
Harryman, Sophia			3	6
Harryman, William of George			1	3
Harryman, Wm. of Thomas-pt. Richardsons Forest		48	1	1
Hillen, Solomon	pt. Hazard	200		
	Privilege	331		
	Shoemakers Hall	150	2	6
Hillen, Thomas	Philemons Lot	nil	1	1
Hess, Valentine			2	3
Hickman, Lawrence			2	5
Hillenger, Michael			3	4
Holbrooks, Amos			2	5
Holbrooks, Jno.	(Bachelor)			
Hudson, Jonathan	pt. Sophias Garden Regulated-33			
Ireland, Richard			4	6
Ivory, John	pt. Norwich		5	7
Jackson, Henry			2	7
Jamison, Enos			2	5
Jarman, Benjamin	pt. Sophies Garden	100	3	6
Johnson, Benjamin			3	5
Johnson, Ephraim			4	6
Johnson, Jno.	pt. Sophias Garden Regulated-43		3	6
Johnson, Joseph	pt. Mount Hase	49 1/2	2	6
Johnson Sarah	pt. Mount Hase	49	0	1
Johnson, Thomas			3	7
Johnson, Wm. Sr.	Farvers Favour	100	5	9
Jones, Susanna	(Pauper)		0	2
King, William	pt. Norwich			
Langton, Joseph	pt. Mount Hase & pt. Privilege-210		3-?	6
Long, Jno.	pt. Dixons	136		
	Rocky Point	11 1/2		
	pt. Privilege	250	4	8
Long, Robert	pt. Sheredines Bottom	200		
Lynox, Nathan			4	5
Lyston, Jas.	pt. Privilege	450		
Markey, William	(Bachelor) Security was Robert Long			
Mattox, William			2	4

1783 TAX LIST OF BALTIMORE COUNTY, MARYLAND
Back River Lower Hundred

Owner	Tract Name	# Acres	Free Males	Total White Inhabitants
Merritt, Jas.	(Pauper)		4	7
Merryman, Cage (Micajah?)	Ensors Study	270		
	pt. Dear Bit	62 1/2		
	surplus land	20		
Merryman, Elijah	pt. Stoney Hills	41		
Merryman, Nicholas	pt. Chevy Chase	200		
	Manors Privilege	80		
Miller, Joseph	(Pauper)		2	3
Moale, John	Stumbling Block	334		
Moore, Nicholas	name unknown	163		
Morris, Joseph	(Pauper)		1	3
Morris, Robert	Gays Inspection	770		
(manager for Mr. Hudson)				
Morris, William	pt. Stansburys Inheritance	275		
	pt. Mount Hase	25		
Mulberry, John			2	3
Mummer, David	pt. Kingsbury Resurveyed	200		
	pt. Sheredines Bottom	50	2	3
Nitzer, John	pt. Sophias Garden Regulated	50	3	6
Norwood, Nicholas	pt. Dear Bit	110		
Oram, Henry	pt. Richardsons Forest	81	6	10
Parlett, David	pt. Smiths Chance	50	1	1
Parlett, Joshua	pt. Smiths Chance	50	1	1
Parlett, Martin	pt. Parletts Fancy	50	1	1
Parlett, Rachel				1
Parlett, Sarah	Parletts Fancy	50		1
Parlett, William			3	4
Partridge, Dominic B.	pt. Balistone	150	3	6
Patterson, John	(Bachelor) Security was Joseph Stansbury			
Patterson, Margaret	(Pauper)		1	3
Patterson, William	(Bachelor) Security was Joseph Stansbury			
Pawling, Robert			1	4
Peckwood, Samuel	(Bachelor)			
Pennington, Jas.	(Pauper)		2	4
Petty, Jno.			2	6
Petty, Orris	pt. Bitchdons? Delight	80	1	3
Porter, Jesse	pt. Double Trouble	100	2	4
Porter, John & Robert & father	pt. Double Trouble	59		
	Danby	700	4	8
Porter, Robert (see John)				
Porter, Robert Jr.			1	1

1783 TAX LIST OF BALTIMORE COUNTY, MARYLAND
Back River Lower Hundred

Owner	Tract Name	# Acres	Free Males	Total White Inhabitants
Potter, Jno.	(Bachelor)			
Pratt, Roger Horas	pt. Stansburys Inheritance	67		
Raven, Rachel	(Pauper)		1	4
Rebout, Ann	(Pauper)		1	4
Renshaw, Jas.	(Bachelor)			
Renshaw, Joseph	pt. Sophias Garden Regulated	174	1	6
Renshaw, Joseph Jr.			2	4
Renshaw, Samuel	(Bachelor)			
Richards, Isaac			2	5
Richards, Jno.	pt. Egypt	73		
Richards, Jon'n.	pt. Dear Bit	109	2	3
Ridgely, Charles	pt. Bonds Lot Enlarged	535		
Rimmer, Jno.			6	8
Roberts, Levin	(Pauper)		2	3
Roberts, Thomas			3	8
Rollings, Ab'm.			2	4
Rollings, William			3	7
Rush/Ruth, Richard	(Pauper)		3	3
Rush, William			1	5
Sanders, Benj'n.			3	7
Shakespear, Saml.			3	5
Shaw, Sabro	(Pauper)		3	4
Sims, Thomas			1	2
Sindell, Phillip (no separate entry; Security for Wm. Warrington)				
Sindall, Saml. Sr.	pt. Dear Bit	62 1/2		
	surplus land	20	3	5
Sindell, William			2	3
Smith, Charles	(Pauper)		1	2
Smith, William	pt. Broads Improvement	170	1	2
Spicer, Ab'm.	(Bachelor) Security was Jno. Harryman Jr.			
Stansbury, Benjamin				
Stansbury, Charles			3	4
Stansbury, David	(Bachelor)			
Stansbury, Dixon	pt. Balistone	117		
	Balistones Support	33		
Stansbury, Isaac	(Bachelor)			
Stansbury, Jno.	pt. Dixon	200		
	Dixons Relief	125		
	Stansburys Vedsmight?	8		
	Timber Swamp	196		
	Stoney Point	7 1/2		
	Millers Island	130	2	3

1783 TAX LIST OF BALTIMORE COUNTY, MARYLAND
Back River Lower Hundred

Owner	Tract Name	½ Acres	Free Males	Total White Inhabitants
Stansbury, Jno. Dixon			2	4
Stansbury, Jno. E.	(Bachelor)			
Stansbury, Joseph			1	6
Stansbury, Luke			2	8
Stansbury, Richard	(Bachelor)			
Stansbury, Richardson	pt. Balistone	100	3	8
Stansbury, Thos. Sr.	pt. Franklins Purchase	641		
	Parishes Neglect	68		
	Longs Addition	14		
	Lukes Goodwill	111		
Stansbury, Tobias	pt. Stansburys Inheritance	720		
Stansbury, William	Strife	268	3	4
Stifer, William	(Pauper)		1	4
Stinchcomb, Aquilla	pt. Paradise Regained	443	2	6
Taylor, Jno.	(Bachelor) Security was Joseph Carter			
Taylor, Joseph	Continuance	888		
	Taylors Addition	718		
	Darley Hall	1	2	2
Taylor, Richard			7	12
Taylor, Samuel			6	12
Thompson, Jane	(Pauper)			2
Thompson, Moses			1	2
Thompson, William Jr.	(Bachelor)			
Todd, Nicholas			2	4
Todd, Thomas	pt. Sophias Garden Regulated-57			
Toppin, Thomas	(Bachelor) Security was Aquilla Stinchcomb			
Trinsham, Henry	(Pauper)		1	4
Trotten, Susanna	Gosicks Folly	50		
Wall, Michael			1	3
Wallage, Jas.	(Pauper)		1	4
Warrington, Wm.	(Bachelor) Security was Philip Sindell			
Watts, Edward A.	pt. Hopewell	70	4	6
Wheeler, Solomon	name unknown	25		
White, Luke	Hap Hazard	93	2	5
White, Luke of John	(Bachelor) Security was Luke White			
Wigley, Edward	(Bachelor)			
Wigley, Isaac			2	4
Willeme, Geo. Averhart	(Bachelor)			
Willeme, Jno. Fred'k.	(Bachelor)			
Willeme, Peter	(Bachelor)			
Williamson, William	(Pauper)		1	3
Willmoth, Henry	(Pauper)		1	4

1783 TAX LIST OF BALTIMORE COUNTY, MARYLAND
Back River Lower Hundred

Owner	Tract Name	# Acres	FREE MALES	Total White Inhabitants
Wilson, Nicholas			1	4
Annis, Joshua	(Pauper)		4	6
Baker, Thomas	(Pauper)		1	2
Bryan, Wm.	(Pauper)		3	6
Bush, Ruth	(Pauper)		1	4
Clark, Jas.	(Pauper)		2	4
Clay, Elizabeth	(Pauper)			1
Clay, Jno.	(Pauper)		1	4
Collins, Timothy	(Pauper)		1	4
Cow, William	(Bachelor) Security was Greenbury Cow			
Croker, Thos.	(Pauper)		2	6
Duff, Jno.	(Pauper)		1	2
Ford, Jno.	(Bachelor)			
Gatch, Benjamin	(Bachelor)			

BALTIMORE EAST HUNDRED

Owner	Whites #Males	#Females	Owner	Whites #Males	#Females
Arnold, Widow		1	Brown, James		
Armstrong, David			Bufort, Rebecca (P)		
Adams, Jno.			Boyer, Jno	1	1
Allen Robert (P)	2	2	Bryson, James		
Alford, Jno. (P)	2	3	Buchanan, Mat'w. (P)	2	
Askew, Wm.			Brereton, Thomas	4	1
Apple, Christn			Bull, Amos	2	2
Asquith, William	3	4	Brown, Jno.	7	4
Berry & Jackson			Barry, Lwellin	2	2
Bailer, William			Brown Fran's.		2
Buck, Jno	3	2	Blush, Joseph (P)	1	3
Bradshaw, Rich	1	3	Beard, Pattie (P)		3
Burtle, Jno	1	2	Ballard, Robert	2	3
Beach, Widow (P)			Boon, Joseph		
Bolton, Franc	2	2	Boyer, George		
Bowers, Jno (P)			Bowley, Daniel		
Burn, Mich'l	1	2	Bond, Jno.		
Bentle, Martin			Buchanan Ellinor		
Bredenbough, Felty (P)	3	1	Casey, Robert		
Bast, Jno (P)	6	2	Corbin, Edward (P)	2	3
Bradley, Thomas (P)	1	4	Craig, Robert (P)	2	3
Britto? Bott? (P)	1	1	Collogan, Michael (P)	1	4

1783 TAX LIST FOR BALTIMORE COUNTY, MARYLAND
Baltimore East Hundred

Owner	# White Male	# White Female	Owner	# White Male	# White Female
Cunningham, James (P)	2	5	Dawson, Martha	2	2
Cummings, Jno (P)	2	4	Davis, Francis	4	2
Cromwell, Philomon			Dowsbury, Jas.	1	1
Clark, Jacob (P)	1	2	Dalling, Frank (P)	4	4
Carter, Richard	1	2	Dennis, William (P)	2	
Clous, Wm.			Dow, Thomas		
Constable, Thomas	11	5	Deaver, Jno.		
Cromwell, Richard			Develbiss, Geo.		
Coleman, Andrew			Edwards, James	1	1
Clark, Joseph (P)	4	2	Ensor, Abraham		
Christie, Zacha. (P)	1	2	Evans, William	2	3
Calver, William	2	4	Fanton, Cornelius (P)	1	3
Croshes, Philip	1	1	Fisher, Daniel (P)	2	3
Chilcote, Robert			France, Abraham	1	3
Constable	1	2	Gorshug, David		
Chaddock, Sarah (P)	4	1	Gaddis, James	1	1
Chunks, Jos.			Gantin, William (P)	2	1
Cole, Samuel	4	2	Graham, William		
Cysler, Christr.	1	1	Gleaves, Elizabeth (P)	1	6
Cole, Fred'k.	5	2	Griffin, Henry (P)	1	1
Cole, Geo.	1		Gibbs, James (P)	2	3
Frederick Cole was Security			Griffith, Isaac (P)	2	5
Capeman & May	5	2	Green, Isaac (P)	4	6
Cox, Mary			Grant, Alexander	1	1
Cooler, Jas. (P)	1	4	Gorsug, Nicholas		
Drown, Thos. (P)	3	2	Gorsug, Jno.		
Doctors Livingsworth & Boyd			Gorsug, Charles		
Dadmore, Christr.	1	1	Griffith Nathan		
Dunkin, Jacob	1	2	Garrison, Job		
Dowson, Chas. (P)	2	2	Galick Jo. & Cooper	3	6
Donaldson, Joseph			Green, Vincent		
Davey, Geo.	6	4	Gordon, Davey		
Dickson, Thos.	1	4	Grant Fielder or Col Loyd		
Dawes, Josiah			Grisler, Christian		
Dulany, Dan'l.			Griffith, Benjamin	4	6
Davis, Robert			Gittings, James		
Davey, Alexander			Holler, Francis	1	3
Davis, Job	8	1	Hanson, Edward		
Delsher Jno. & Christr.	4	1	Humphries, Cato		
Davis, William	5	2	Hon, Jno.	2	2
Dunn Anthony	2	2	Hackerman, George	1	2
Dorling, Monos	2	1	Hughes, Andrew	2	2

1783 TAX LIST FOR BALTIMORE COUNTY, MARYLAND
Baltimore East Hundred

Owner	# White Male	# White Female	Owner	# White Male	# White Female
Allison, John (P)	1	2	Long, Robert (P)	2	3
Hornby, Walter (P)	3	1	Lawrence, Jacob		
Hussel, George			Lawrence, Ferdinand (P)	1	2
Hughes, Christopher			Leeke, Peter	1	2
Hartman, Jacob	2	2	Liston, William (P)	3	2
Husk, Bennett			Letzinger, Peter	2	1
Hollingsworth, Jesse			Lynch, Patrick		
Hackett, Betsey			Litzinger, Henry (P)	3	2
Haywood, William	4	5	Litzinger, ? Michael (P)	3	1
Hook, Fred & Ann Coorrod	4	5	Lemmon, Richard		
Hale, George (P)	2	2	Liscomb, John	1	1
Honley, Mary (P)		5	Long, James		
Holston, Robert (P)	2	1	Lemmon, John		
Hutchinson, Robert	3	2	Lindenberger, George		
Hughes, Thomas (P)	1	2	Lane, Nathaniel		
Hammond, Wm. Merchant			Love, Miles		
Horner, Margaret			Levi, Benjamin		
Hillen Solomon			Matthews, Samuel		
Hoffman, Andrew			Miller, John	1	1
Heatherington, James (P)	2	1	Morris, William (P)	2	1
Hanson, Amon			Mullan, James	2	1
Harrison, William			Mumma, Christian	1	2
Hamilton, Gardner, Jr.			McDonnell, John	1	1
Ingram, Mrs. (P)	1	4	Milliken, John (P)	1	3
Jones, John (P)	1	1	McFaddon, Capt. James		
Jones, Solomon	3	3	Myers, Fred'k. & Sloler		
Jordan, Henry	2	2	Moore, Nicholas		
Jarrett, Mary			Mumma, David (P)	2	2
Jackson, Isaac	6	5	Myers, Jacob (P)	2	3
Johnson, Dr.			McPhersons, Malcom (P)	3	4
Joyce, Joseph	1	1	Marsh, Nicholas (P)	3	1
Jeer, John	1	3	Meale, John	1	1
Jacobs, William			Matthews, Richard	1	2
Jeffereys, John			Moore, Widow (P)		
Johnson, John			McCabe, John	2	2
Killinger, John (P)	2	3	Manahan, James	2	2
Keller, Jacob (P)	1	1	Matthews, George	3	2
Keneday, Marea		2	Mansfield, Jemima (P)	2	4
Katohey, Thomas	1	1	Moale, John		
Keller, Widow			Merryman, Elijah		
Kelso, James			Moore, David		

1783 TAX LIST FOR BALTIMORE COUNTY, MARYLAND
Baltimore East Hundred

Owner	# White Male	# White Female	Owner	# White Male	# White Female
Mullan, Patrick (P)			✓ Roe, Walter		
Marshall, James (P)			Reed, John (listed twice)		
Mackey, Ebenezer	1		Reese, Daniel (P)	4	1
Merryman, Micajah			Riely, George (P)	2	3
Moore Ann (P)		3	Ross, James	4	4
Molsby, John (P)	1	2	Rettenberg, Lewis	4	1
Messer, Smith (P)	2	1	Riely, Conrad		
McCandles, George			Ricks, Robert	1	4
Merryman, Nicholas			Richie, William (P)	2	2
Myers, Frederick			✓Robison, Joseph (P)	2	7
Merryman, John			✓ Riddle, William (P)	3	2
Murray, John Collier			Riely, John		
Moore, Capt. Thomas			Rider, John	2	1
Moore, Widow (P)	4	4	Reams, Stophel		
Mull, Jacob	2	5	✓ Reese, John	3	1
Muday, James	2	2	✓ Russell, Thomas		
Morris, Samuel			Runnells, William	1	1
Moore, William			✓ Ridgely, Charles of Wm.		
Fitzgerald, Robert	1	1	✓ Riely, Charles		
Nice, Dolly			Ross, James		
Noon, William	1	1	Ryan, Dennis		
Nailor, John	1	3	Stansbury, Jacob (Bachelor) Sec. Edw. Dorsey		
Neel, William			Strider, Joseph (P)	3	3
Nox, William	3	3	Smith, James		
Nicholson, Benjamin			Scott, Abraham		
Olive, Mark (P)	2	3	Speck, John	4	2
Owens, Samuel (miller)			Savage Mr.		
Owens, Samuel (merchant)			Sly, John		
Peleg, William	2	2	Sullivan, Bright (P)	2	3
Pauley, Christian	1	1	Shock, Christian (P)	1	1
Pool, William			Stevens, Daniel	4	2
Philips, Henry	2	2	Shilling, Michael		
Pratt, Capt.			Sank, John (P)	5	4
Price, Samuel			Smith Widow of Conrad		
✓Philpot, Bryan	1	3	Stuart, Hugh	3	3
Porketts, Michael			Silvester, John	2	1
Pearson, Samuel			Sylvia, Joseph	1	2
✓Patterson, John			Slaymaker, John		
Roberts, Jamima (P)		3	Steigar, Andrew		
Reed, John (P)	3	1	Smith, William (P)	1	1
✓ Ridgely, Charles			Sumbolt, Belcher (P)	3	2

1783 TAX LIST OF BALTIMORE COUNTY, MARYLAND
Baltimore East Hundred

Owner	# White Male	# White Female	Owner	# White Male	# White Female
Shriek, John			Thornbery, William	1	
Snider, Paul (P)	3	1	Vaun, Isaac	1	4
Shilling, Michael (P)	1	3	Willson, William		
Stchudy, Nicholas			Winks, Joseph (P)	3	2
Speck, William (P)	4	2	Weaver, Peter	4	1
Smith, Mary (P)		3	Woodcock, Robert		
Sterling, James			Wainor, Widow		
Spear, William			Welch, John	1	2
Spear, John			Williams, Charles	3	5
Scorey, William			Wells, Cyprian		
Seagersley, Martin			West, Jacob	1	2
Stewart, Sarah			Worthington, Samuel	1	2
Shepherd, John	1	2	West, Mary (P)		2
Thompson, John	1	1	Wilkinson, Young	2	1
Traves, Col.			Walter, Hezekiah	4	6
Tucker, Thomas (P)	2	2	Wispaw, Martin (P)	1	2
Tumbledown, Henry	1	2	Weaver, D niel	3	3
Taylor, John	1	2	Webster, Widow		
Tuckett, John (Bachelor) Sec. John Hon			Wheeler, Isaac (P)	1	4
Treagle, George	3	2	Wall, Thomas	2	4
Smith, Wm. to Esq. Shepherd			Worthington, Henry	3	2
Trippier, Joseph			Walker, Joseph	3	1
Tripolete, Mary			Willis, George	2	2
Yiever, Philip	5	3	Wertenberg, Lewis		
Yates, Thomas			Young, John		

A LIST OF GROUND RENTS PAID TO JOHN CORNTHWAIT, ESQ.

Abraham France	George Diat	Elish Tyson & A. Davey	Elisha Tyson
Jacob Hartman	Francis Peper	Peter Littig	John Constable
Henry Hartman	Walter Simpson	George Hassey	Henry Lorah
Lewellin Barrey	James Griffeth	Andrew Ellicott & Co.	John Ward
Isiah Jackson	Jacob Small	John & Andrew Ellicott	Richard Bradshaw
Peter Leddick	Caleb Hall	Nathan Griffith &	James Davidson
Walter Simpson		Joshua Carey	Joseph Trippier

A LIST OF GROUND RENTS PAID TO JOHN MOALE, ESQ.

Walter Hornby	James Green	John Tolly Young	Stephen Bayhon
Conrad Riely	Benjamin Ford	Morris Baker	Wm. Wilson
David Moore	Caleb Brown	Robert Chilcote	Abel Headington
Wm. Fus	William Carter	George Haile	Michael Curgan
John Ensor of Abrm.	Arch'd. Simpson	Henry Jordon	John Cunningham
Jacob West	John Riely	Nicholas Marsh	Peter Slimmer

1783 TAX LIST OF BALTIMORE COUNTY, MARYLAND
Delaware Upper Hundred

The 1783 Tax List, found in the Scharf collection, at the Maryland Historical Society shows the hundred contained 48,053 acres; 191 white males including the poll taxes, and 991 whites.

Owners	Tract Name	# Acres	Free Males	Total white Inhabitants
Arnold, Joseph	pt. Arnolds Harbour	135	1	10
Arnold, Benjamin	pt. Arnolds Harbour	130		
	pt. Rochester	100	1	9
Anderson Jane	Bucks Park	50		2
Amey, Phillip			1	10
Aston, Peter			1	6
Arnold Jacob			1	3
Buckingham Zale	Cambells Search	155	1	4
Buckingham, John	Bucking	66	1	8
Beach, Ann				2
Brothers, Francis	Hammonds Meadows	100	1	8
Beasman, John	Stinchcombs Reserve	100	1	3
Botts, John	pt. Rochester	100	1	7
Bennett, Samuel	Sandy Bottom	140		
	pt. Wages Trust	67 1/2		
	pt. Wages Trust	13 3/4		
	pt. Watson Trust	30	1	9
Boring, William	pt. Escape	58		
	pt. Hog Range	50		
	Twins' Purchase	16	1	10
Bailey, William	Williams Intent	60	1	8
Bates, John	Marshalls Desire	23 3/4	1	4
Bryan, Thomas	Willmotts Mountain	50	1	4
Barnes, Dorsey	Morgans Tent Reserveyed	132	1	6
Barnes, Adam	Basemans Discovery (sic)	144	1	6
Beasman, Joseph	Basemans Discovery "	380	1	7
Beasman, Thomas	Basemans Discovery "	450	1	5
Buckingham Zebediah			1	5
Buckingham, Benjamin Sr.	pt. Bucking	200		
	pt. Teagues Ramble	37	2	6
Buckingham, Obediah	pt. Teagues Ramble	60	1	1
Buckingham, John			1	8
Beaver, John	pt. Rochester	200	1	4
Brooks, Clement	Brooks Adventure	500		
Brasher, Rezin	Shipley's Choice	50	1	7
Baker, Indimion			1	5
Bennett, Elisha	pt. Watsons Trust	200		
	Bennetts Park	32	1	3
Cook, John	pt. Watsons Trust	83		7
	pt. The Escape	25	1	

1783 TAX LIST OF BALTIMORE COUNTY, MARYLAND
Delaware Upper Hundred

Owners	Tract Name	# Acres	Free Males	Total White Inhabitants
Bennett, Mary				
Bennett, Thomas	pt. Watsons Trust	52 1/2		
	pt. Wages Trust	53		
	Addition to Watsons Trust	47 1/2		
	Everitts Friendship	26		
	Marshall's Desire	32		
	pt. Watsons Trust	33	2	13
Buchanan, William	pt. Winsor Forrest	1774		
	Davis' Farm	350		
	pt. Good Neighbourhood	188		
	Thomas' Folly	60		
	pt. Johns Chance	28		
Bardell, Charles	pt. Barnes' Level	50		
Bell, William	pt. White Oak Bottom	130		
	Matthews Forrest	50		
	pt. White Oak Bottom	165		
	Caladonia	2500		
	pt. Bucks Forrest	229		
	Timber Neck	25		
Bowers Daniel	name unknown			
Conner, James	Sewell Park	20		
	Bucks Park	10		
	Beasmans Discovery	53	1	5
Chinnowith, William	pt. Rochester	150		
Carrs, John	pt. Williams Defence	18 1/2		
Cook, Ann	Cooks Desire	146	1	5
Connaway, Charles	Connaways Venture Improved	200		
	Beasmans Discovery	138	1	7
Connaway, John	pt. Connaways Venture	150		
	pt. Benjamins Discovery	62	1	3
Cross, John	pt. Carrickfergus	75	1	4
Crisswell, Eliza	pt. Barnes Level	48		3
Cross, Robert	Mattocks Choice	30	1	6
Crisswell, Richard	pt. Caladonia	302	1	8
Crisswell, William	pt. Bucks Range	88	1	2
Crayoner, Stophel	name unknown	411	2	8
Chapman, Rezin			1	11
Cook, John of Thomas	pt. Bakers Discovery	72		
	Welshes Discovery	115	1	9
Dorsey, James			1	5
Dorsey, Sarah	Forrest Level	172		2

1783 TAX LIST OF BALTIMORE COUNTY, MARYLAND
Delaware Upper Hundred

Owners	Tract Name	# Acres	Free Males	Total White Inhabitants
Davis, Nathaniel	Charles Luck	65		
	Wilmotts Meadows	210	1	12
Dorsey, G. Orlando			1	2
Dilling, James	pt. Bakers Discovery	130		
	Surplus	5	1	4
Deaver, Philip	pt. Upper Malborough	170 1/2	1	5
Dick, James	Edenborough	2685		
	Giest Silvania	120		
	Dowleys Range	100		
Davis Robert	name unknown	10		
Elder, Elijah	Bucks Park	151		
	Adams Garden	40		
	name unknown	30	1	5
Evans, Thomas	Turks Range	50	1	5
Edwards, John			1	7
Franklin, Charles	pt. Forrest Levell	190 3/4	1	5
Frissell, Abraham			1	6
Fisher, Peter	Georges Lott	79	1	2
Frissell, John	name unknown	115	1	11
Fowler, John	Denmark	240	1	10
Finlay, Thomas			1	5
Farver, Adam	pt. Bakers Discovery	100	1	3
Frissell, John			1	3
Gorsuch, Nathan	pt. Bakers Discovery	100	1	5
Gladman, John			1	8
Gough, D. Henry	pt. Flag Meadow	1315		
Grahams, heirs	pt. Caladonia	2470		
Goodwin, Lloyd	Shadricks Last Shift	420		
Gorsuch, John	name unknown	100		
Griffith, Richard	Cross's Chance	23 3/4	1	7
Gorsuch Nathan of Lov.	Add. to Plumb Tree Bottom	39		
	Add. to Plumb Tree Bottom	30		
	Morgans Tent	200	1	5
Gorsuch, Thomas			1	5
Goodwin, Henry	Isaacs Retirement	140	1	9
Gaughn, William	name unknown	80	1	7
Gladman, Michael			1	3
Hanes Anthony	Hawkins Fancy	276	1	4
Hudson, Robert	Hutsons Forrest	252		
Hewit, Edward	pt. Sandy Bottom	260		
	Wages Trust	49	1	7

1783 TAX LIST OF BALTIMORE COUNTY, MARYLAND
Delaware Upper Hundred

Owners	Tract Name	# Acres	Free Males	Total White Inhabitants
Hawkins, John	Peach Brandy Forrest	765		
Hook, Michael			1	1
Hays, John	pt. Rochester	100		
Hewit, Rachel			1	5
Horton, Isaac			1	6
Hooke, Jacob, Sr.	Carickfergus	182 1/2	1	3
Hooke, William			1	6
Hooke, Jacob, Jr.	Dunkers Lott	148		
	pt. Georges	89 1/2	1	3
Hawkins, Joseph	pt. Peach Brandy Forrest	100	1	7
Howard, Joshua (Quarter)	pt. Rich Meadows	200		
	pt. Strawberry Patch	30		
	Surplus lands	83	1	3
Huff, Ludwick			1	4
Haden, William	pt. Friendship Completed	134	1	7
Hooker, Barney	pt. Hookers Meadows	140	1	7
Hooker, Aquilla	pt. Flag Meadows	105 1/2	1	1
Hooker, Samuel	pt. Hookers Meadow	166	1	4
Hooker, Richard	pt. Flag Meadow	105	1	1
Hudson, Jonathan	pt. Deer Park	392		
	Joshua's Gift	57		
	name unknown	160		
Jordon, Robert			1	7
Jacobs, John	Stevensons Manor	900		
	pt. Caledonia	270	1	3
Jordon, Wm. & Thos.	pt. Cold Saturday	50	2	3
Jacks, Thomas	Lowry's Lott	50	1	2
Jervis, Philip	pt. Upper Malborough	345	1	5
Jones, Thos. & Co.	Cotts Mine	30		
Kneff, Henry	Friendship Compleat	200	1	9
Knewcom, Mary	Conners Delight	120	1	6
Kelly, Charles			1	7
K... William of Charles			1	7
Love, Miles	pt. Rochester	100		
Lonsell, George			1	4
Lane, Daniel	Game Plenty	100	1	6
Lindsay, John			1	12
Lavely, Philip			1	7
Long, John	pt. Flag Meadow	100		
Lux, George	Newks Hill	601 1/2		
	Mount Pisga	699		
	pt. Stoney Crossway	100		

1783 TAX LIST OF BALTIMORE COUNTY, MARYLAND
Delaware Upper Hundred

Owners	Tract Name	# Acres	Free Males	Total White Inhabitants
Lux, Coll. Darby	Barbadoes	880		
Lucas, James			1	6
Logsdon, Lawrence	pt. Donmark	100		
	pt. Peach Brandy	180		
	name unknown	20	2	11
Lawrence, Benjamin	Rich Meadow	141		
	Strawberry Patch	80		
	Mill Place	37		
	Bakers Discovery	202		
	Point Esprite	171		
	& Surplus	83		
	Sidling Hill	14 3/4		
	Bite the Biter	15 1/4	1	8
Logsdon, William			1	4
Logue, James	Peggy's Chance	40	1	9
Mackelfresh, David	pt. The Escape	50		
	pt. New Tavern	30		
	David's Hope	7	1	8
Major, Robert	pt. Beasmans Discovery	50	1	8
McAllister, Robert	Indian Town	60		
	pt. Buck's Goodwill	99		
	Stevensons Manor	66		
	Herriford	36 1/2		
	Mattocks Folly	25		
	School Lott	3 3/4		
	pt. Bucks Forrest	75	1	8
Miller, Thomas	pt. Bucks Goodwill	96	1	7
Merryman, Nicholas			1	3
Merryman, Samuel Sr.	Cumberland	342		
	pt. Stevensons Manor	100		
Merryman, Samuel Jr.			1	6
McGee, James			1	6
Manning, Samuel Jr.	pt. White Oak Bottom	150	1	5
Mitchel, John	pt. Peach Brandy Forrest	50	1	3
Moore, Gay John	name unknown	125		
Owings, Richard of Saml.	Amam Inheritance	14		
	Pouths Gain	34		
	Rich Meadows	20		
	Richards Disappointment	5		
	pt. Rich Meadows	207		
	Point Espril	141		
	Surplus land	83	1	6

1783 TAX LIST OF BALTIMORE COUNTY, MARYLAND
Delaware Upper Hundred

Owners	Tract Name	# Acres	Free Males	Total White Inhabitants
Owings, Betsey	pt. Rich Meadows	400		
	pt. Rochester	127		8
Ouslar, Ely	Bucks Range	170		
	Bucks Park	13	1	10
Ogg, Helen	Bashan	512		
	pt. Caledonia	111	1	6
Owings, Richard	Owings Choice	120		
	pt. Rochester	100		
	Timber Bottom	44		
	Scheming Defeated	74	1	2
Owings, George			1	3
Owings, Samuel	Surveyors Discovery	615		
Phillips, Thomas	pt. Wages Trust	92		
	pt. Watsons Trust	35		
	pt. Marshalls Desire	165		
	pt. Marshalls Desire	68		
	pt. Wages Trust	50		
	Bennets Grievance	23		
	pt. Watsons Trust	41		
	Dispute Ended	4	2	13
Parrish Wm. of John	pt. Flag Meadow	50	1	8
Pattman, Robert			1	4
Plumb, John	pt. Rochester	300		
Rooles Thomas	Arnolds Desire	206		
Ridgely, Matthew	Stepney Cross Way	500		
Stocksdale, Edmund	Add. to McLanes Hills	74		
	Stocksdales Grove	16		
	Edwards Venture	25		
	McLanes Venture	50		
	Stocksdales Provision	117	1	8
Stocksdale, Zeb'h			1	3
Sellman, William	pt. Everitts Progress	100		
	Abners Delight	12		
	pt. Johns Chance	192	1	10
Selman, Jonathan	Browns Sharp	249		
Stevenson, John	pt. Arnolds Desire	157		
Stringer, Richard	name unknown	228		
Selman, Johnsa	Warbore Hills	779		
Schooles, John	pt. Caladonia	100	1	11
Stevenson, Henry	pt. Rich Meadows	273		
	Canaan	150		
	pt. Bucks Range	244	1	2

1783 TAX LIST OF BALTIMORE COUNTY, MARYLAND
Delaware Upper Hundred

Owners	Tract Name	# Acres	Free Males	Total White Inhabitants
Sellman, John	Neighbours Friendship	150	1	8
Selby, Mordecai			1	3
Smith, Mary	pt. Upper Malborough	100		
Stembler, Nicholas	name unknown	72	1	5
Selvey, W. Jas.	pt. Bonnets Park	92		
	pt. Watsons Trust	55	1	11
Shipley, Peter of Adam	name unknown	55	1	5
Stevenson, Dr. John	Deer Park & Trouting Streams-2699		1	1
Stout William			1	7
Smith, Eliza	Smiths Fancy	15	1	3
Stains, Thomas	pt. Bonds Forrest	47	1	7
Tevis, Nathaniel	pt. Tivis Chance	111		
	Peters Leavings	15 3/4		
	Little More	8	1	10
Trash, Jacob	pt. Peach Brandy Forrest	50	1	7
Tinfill, Godfrey			1	5
Tipton, Aquilla	pt. Hookers Meadows	111	1	4
Tennor, John			2	8
Talbott, Edward Jr.	Wilsons Range	100		
	pt. Long Trusted	444 1/2	1	6
Tivis, Peter	pt. Tivis's Chance	111		
	Fathers Gift	25	1	11
Thompson, Henry	pt. Fellsdale	100		
Tevis, Robert Jr.	pt. Tevis Chance	111		
	Costly	9	1	1
Urills heirs	Cockermouth	400		
Wertian, Charles	Stevens Folly	200	1	4
Wheeler, Edward	Buttons Adventure	40	1	7
Willson, John			1	6
Welsh, John	Perseverance	869		
	Add. to Perseverance	43 1/2		
	Milford Enlarged	92		
	Kildare	50		
	Arabia Petre Enlarged	604		
	Last Choice	30		
	Arabia Felix	50		
	Modena	52		
	pt. Good Neighbourhood	314		
	pt. Upper Marlborough	737	3	
Willson Charles	-		1	4
Wells, Benjamin	pt. Rochester	233		

-19-

1783 TAX LIST OF BALTIMORE COUNTY, MARYLAND
Delaware Upper Hundred

Owners	Tract Name	# Acres	Free Males	Total White Inhabitants
Wallton, John	pt. Bond's Forrest	96	1	6
Willson, William			1	11
Wells, Benjamin	pt. Rochester	233		
Walker, John	pt. Rochester	114	1	7
Wages, William	name unknown	70	1	9
Woolery, Stephen			1	4
Williams, Benjamin			1	7
Williams, Benjamin Jr.			1	3
Willmot, Richard	Willmots Wilderness	133		
	Deep Valley	325		
	Willmots Mountain	50		
Willmot, Robert	Willmots Meadows	203		
Willmot, John	pt. Rochester	450		

PAUPERS

Names	# Males	Total	Names	# Males	Total
James Asboury	1	2	William Gosnell	1	3
Anthony Arnold	1	2	Rezin Hawkins	1	6
James Bachedlor	1	2	Mary Jacobs		4
Martin Beaver	1	3	Henry Lynderman	1	3
Joshua Bennett	1	1	William Lard	1	3
Thomas Brothers	1	9	William McLane	1	6
Elizabeth Clark		6	John Murphy	2	7
Sarah Cole		3	Joseph Peacock	1	5
			Samuel Roach	1	2

Single Men	Securities		Single Men	Securities	
Wm. Boring Jr.	Wm. Boring Sr.	1-1	Geo. Buckingham	Benj. Buckingham	1-1
Wm. Cambell	Robert Major	1-1	Ben Buckingham Jr.	Benj. Buckingham	1-1
Benj. Crisswell	Benj. Ogg	1-1	Isaac Cook	Poll Tax	1-1
James Crisswell	Benj. Crisswell	1-1	Danl. Davis	Stephel Craymer	1-1
John Farver	Adam Farver	1-1	Conrad Hyle	John Teanor	1-1
Edw. Hewit Jr.	Edw. Hewit	1-1	Henry Kneff Jr.	Henry Kneff	1-1
Joshua Owings			John Philips	Thos. Philips	1-1
of Richard	Richard Owings	1-1	William Rice	Saml. Bennett	1-1
Vachel Selman	John Sellman	1-1	John Steal	Nathan Tivis	1-1
Philip Teanor	John Teanor	1-1	Tobias Talbott	Edw. Talbott	1-1

1783 TAX LIST FOR BALTIMORE COUNTY, MARYLAND
Deptford Hundred

Owner	# White Male	# White Female	Owner	# White Male	# White Female
Annells, Skinner			Button, Elias (P)	1	5
Adams, Thomas	1	3	Baitys ? Samuel	3	4
Anderson, Thomas	1	2	Bond and Bennett		
Adams, William			Bryant, Daniel	2	3
Ashpaw, Henry			Bradley, Robert (Ralph Stoney, Security)		
Aikle, James	1	1	Bennett, Thomas		
Blackrote, Henry	2	3	Collins, James	2	2
Bennett, Jane			Corrothers, Robert	2	2
Beachum, William	3	3	Conner, Timothy (P)		
Boyd, James	1	3	Carroll, Marlin		
Britt, Robert	1	1	Corrithwait, John (deceased, his estate)		
Burns, Simon	2	2	Crampton, Derman	1	3
Barlow, John (P)	1	1	Carroll, John		
Burner, John (Wm. Davis Security)			Copes, James (P)	1	3
Button, Margaret		1	Carson, Robert (Peter Wery, security)		
Bole, John	1	2	Corman, Ab'm.		
Baxter, Bernard	1		Calgoe, James	3	1
Brown, John	1	1	Craighead, Jemima	1	3
Brimingham, Christopher	1	3	Clemmons, John (Deceased)	1	2
Barber, James (P)	1	1	Connor, Doctor	1	3
Boss, Adam (P)	1	1	Corwin, W. Marchant		
Boyd, Mary			Clark, Richard	1	1
Bias, Joseph	4	5	Curtin, James	4	2
Bowley, Daniel			Crockett, John & Benj.		
Bernard, John	3	2	Cole, James (P)	3	1
Brown, Mary		7	Crips, Michael	6	3
Beven, Richard	4	4	Connelly, Margaret		5
Boss, Nicholas	2	2	Chambers, Wm.	3	1
Boss, Peter	3	4	Calhoun, James	1	2
Burkett, John	2	2	Colter, John	1	0
Bailey, John			Cockland, Patrick (P)	1	3
Brookman, Jane		2	Conway, Robert	3	4
Brooks, James	3	1	Chapple, John	2	3
Brown, John	1	2	Clark, Butcher	3	4
Buchanan, George			Cooper, Jonas	5	2
Buck, John			Cameron, James	1	3
Bond, Thomas			Carlyle, Charles		
Brown, John (Currier)			Davis, Ann		
Bond, Buckler			Dougherty, Joseph	1	2
Barney, John			Dawson, Jacob	1	3
Brown, Dickson	4	3	Dougherty, John	1	2

1783 TAX LIST FOR BALTIMORE COUNTY, MARYLAND
Deptford Hundred

Owner	# White Male	# White Female	Owner	# White Male	# White Female
Doyl, Mary (P)	1	2	Glynn, William	2	4
Davis, William	6	5	Gibbons, John	1	1
Deshield, Benjamin	5	3	Gordon, Mary		1
Davis, Joseph (P)	1		Gibbons, Jane (P)	1	2
Davis, Widow (P)	2	2	Green, Mary (P)	1	1
Dougherty, John (P)	1	1	Green, Nathaniel		
Dickinson Brittingm.	1	3	Grimes, William (P)	1	2
Dorsey, Edward			Gordon, John		
Davey, Alexander			Garns, William	2	2
Davey & Barney			Garrison, Job		
Dawson, Robert	3	2	Gottier, Edward	3	4
Delaport, W. Merchant	1	1	Green, Joseph		
Davidson, Andrew	1	3	Henderson, Robert	3	4
Donnell, Widow (P)	2	2	Hall, John	1	2
Elliott, Thomas	1	5	Hays, William	5	4
Evans, Henry	5	1	Hollingsworth, Thomas		
Electan, Francis (P)	2	1	Hall, Margaret	3	2
Ensor, Jon'n.	2	1	Hamilton, Ralph		
Errickson, Benjamin			Hannah, Patrick	2	3
Foulger, Frederick			Hellin, David	3	5
Feller, James	3	1	Haff, Robert (Sec. Patrick Honan)		
Foster, James	2	2	Hesam, Robert (P)	2	1
French, Eleanor			Harper, Richard	1	1
Flaugherty, James (Sec. Abel Mitchel)			Hinsom, Mary (P)	2	6
Foye, Michael	4	4	Hopham, William	2	2
Foster, William	1	1	Hughes, John	1	1
Foster, Captain	1	1	Hopkins, John	4	2
Flax, Michael	1	2	Hollingsworth, Jesse		
Forber, James			Hughes, Christopher		
Fell, Wm. Esq.			Hopkins & Willson		
Garts, Charles			Hamilton, Joseph (P)	4	6
Gittings, James			Holmes, James	1	4
Guthery, John	3	2	Higginbottom, John	1	3
Goodwin, William			Hammond, John		
Gorman, Abraham	2	2	Hall, Caleb		
Godman, Samuel	3	2	Hall, Jonathan		
Gurnel Joseph	2	2	Holmes, William (P)	2	2
Griffeth, Benjm.			Hyner, Nicholas	2	3
Grist, Isaac	1	2	Husse & Brownattan	5	3
Grist, George	1		Hensman, Samuel		
Gather, Burges (Sec. Robert Long)			Hammond, William		

-22-

1783 TAX LIST OF BALTIMORE COUNTY, MARYLAND
Deptford Hundred

Owner	# White Male	# White Female	Owner	# White Male	# White Female
Hawkins, James			Louderman, George	4	3
Hellems, George	5	3	Lusha, Andrew	1	1
Jacobs, Wm. of Zachariah			Laurence, Richard	5	2
Johnson, Dr.			Legge, Thos. (Sec. Abraham Inloes)		
Johns, William (P)	5	4	Larkin, Ann (P)		4
Jackson, Abraham	4	9	Lackfingers, Peter		
Johnson, William	8	7	Littig, Peter	6	2
Jacob, William	6	3	Lecky, Richard	2	3
Irwin, Mr. (York Town)	?		Larie, Daniel	2	2
Jones, Capt. Jr.			Larie, Cornelius		
Jones, Capt. Senior			Lavelly, William		
Jones, Capt. Daniel	2	1	Labold, Jacob (P)	2	2
Joyce, Stephen			McKim, Robert & A.V.		
Jaffery, James			Mitchell, Capt. John	3	10
Johnson, Absalom	1	1	Mayson, Abraham	4	2
Inloes, Abram	7	3	McBridge, Mary		
Job, Mr. (P)	4	3	Maxwell, James	2	3
Skeppy, John	1	5	Mathews, James	2	2
Johns, Aquilla	2	4	McLure, John		
Johnson, Thomas	3	4	Minsky, Widow		4
James, George	2	4	Mayson, George (Sec. R. Beaver)		
Johnston, Christian			Mather, John	4	3
James, Hannah			Morrison, Hans		
Kell, Thomas			Morrison, John (cooper)	2	3
K·lly, Thomas (P)	1	2	McBride, Archibald (P)	2	3
Kingsbridge, George	4	4	Mullen, William	1	2
Keysted, Jane		2	McKeever, James		
Kees, Katherine	1	3	Murray, Edward		
Keller, John	1	3	McCausland, Marius		
Kimbo, Joseph (P)	1	2	Morgan, James	5	3
Keener, Melchior			McGuire, Anthony	1	1
Kees, Robert	4	1	McCreery, Wm.		
Langford, Edward	1	3	Morris, William	1	2
Long, Robert	3	3	Morris, Thomas	1	2
Lee, Robert (P)	3	1	Miller, John	2	1
Lemmon, John			Middleton, Joseph		
Littig, Eliza			Middy, John (P)	1	4
Lindsay, Adam			McGurie, Andrew (P)	3	2
Laypole, John			More, Stephen		
Logan, William (P)	1	3	Moss, Abraham		
Leage, James (P)	3	2	McMachan, David		

1783 TAX LIST OF BALTIMORE COUNTY, MARYLAND
Deptford Hundred

Owner	# White Male	# White Female	Owner	# White Male	# White Female
Monk, Henry			Rogers, Philip		
McCullen Robt.(Sec.Edw.Gettier)			Rea, Wm.(Sec.Stoddard)		
Murray, James			Robison, Elijah		
Mays, Mary			Rusk, Adam		
McKeever, William			Rouse, James	4	2
Mitchel, Wm.(Sec.Edw.Gettier)			Right, James	2	3
Myers, Jacob			Rutledge, Thomas		
Mitchel, Abel			Ridge, Jonathan	2	3
McMechan, Patrick (P)	2	4	Rogers, John	1	3
Mitchel John (Back Creek)			Russ, David	1	
McKean Rodorick (Sec.Wm.Williams)			Rus, Christian		
Neel, William			Roe, Walter		
Numle, William (P)	2	5	Robison, George	2	3
Neel, Dennis (P)	1	2	Rus, George	1	2
Owen, John			Ramsey Col. & McMechan		
Osburn, Alex.(a blind man)	2	3	Shaw, Thomas		
Oniel, Henry (Sec.A.Davidson)			Stansbury, Richard		
O Brient, Jacob (P)	1	1	Solman, Deborah	2	5
Onnick, John	4	2	Solman, Wm.	2	4
Pannell, John	1	2	Savory, Wm.		
Pan, Rebekah (P)		3	Rine? Thomas (Sec.Geo.Holems)		
Pringle, Mark			Ricketss David		
Patterson, Robert	1	1	Sheets, John	4	7
Penrice, Mr. (P)	1	1	_____ & Smith		
Patterson, James	2	2	Steward _____		
Patterson, John (P)	1	3	Stranbell Zachariah	2	3
Porter, Lewis	2	1	Stoddard, Seth (Sec.David Stoddard)		
Panon, John	4	2	Sinclaire Frances	2	2
Pine, John	1	1	Sands, John (Sec.Wm.Johnson)		
Peters, Abejah	1	2	Smith Wm. (P)	2	1
Press, Henry			Tschudy Nicholas		
Purviance, Samuel			Tschudy Marlin		
Purviance, Robert			Slater, Wm.		
Parker, Wm. (Sec.A.Lindsay)			Schaeffer, Jacob	5 ?	4
Porter, James (Sec.Jonathan Ridge)			Stoker, _____ (P)	2	3
Powers, Richard	2	2	Sheets, Henry (Sec.Christopher Wasky)		
Patterson Wm. (merchant)			Stoddard David	5	2
Prath, Horace	2	2	Smith, Thorogood		
Rogers, Elizabeth (P)	1	3	Stevens Wm. (P)	2	3
Ross, John	4	3	Smith John Merchant		
Robinson, James (Sec.Mr.Dawson)			Smith Thomas		

1783 TAX LIST OF BALTIMORE COUNTY, MARYLAND
Deptford Hundred

Owner	# White Male	# White Female	Owner	# White Male	# White Female
Stansby, Elizabeth (P)	1	1	Tull, Elijah	2	2
Stansbury, Elijah			Usher, Thomas	4	6
Sterrett, James			Umphries, Wm.	2	1
S_____ William	2	3	Vanderson, Matthew (Sec. Mr. Lawrence)		
Sterrett, John			Vandevote, John	2	2
Steel, Peter	3	2	Van Bibber, Isaac		
Sampson, Jacob	3	2	Van Bibber, Abraham		
Summers, Jacob (P)	2	1	Winning, John	1	2
Sanders, Edward	2	2	Wasky, Christian	7	2
Sollers? Barbara		2	Weaver, John	1	2
Simpson, Ann (P)	1	3	Williamson, David		
Sinclair, Uriah	1	3	Weatherteum, John		
Shoehorn, Mary			Webb Henry		
Shillingberg, Peter	3	4	Welch, Robert	1	1
Stett, George	2	2	Welch, Stephen	1	3
Seiglar, John	1	2	Ward, Capt. Wm.	2	3
Shoffer, John (Sec. Peter Boss)			Wagster, Ijiah		
Smith William			Wannell, Henry	2	3
Shieighley, Michael	2	3	Walker, John	4	3
Speares, Boni	3	1	Wells, Charles		
Sh____ue Nathan	1	1	Woods, John	2	4
Service, Capt. James			Wheatley, John (Single	1	
Smith, Samuel, Col.			Woods, Isaac (Single)	1	
Sutton, Isaac	2	1	Ward, Wm. (Sec. Christian Wasky)		
Spear, William			Willsin John (Sec. James Collins)		
Spear, John			Wester, John		
Shields & Maltison			Werry, Peter	4	5
Stansbury, Tobias	1	1	Waters, Wm.	1	1
Storey, Ralph	4	2	Willaby, Ann	4	4
Tumblinson, Wm.	2	1	Webster, James		
Tool, James			Webster, Samuel		
Tibbett, James	2	1	Wells, Kensington	3	3
Tyler, Littleton	2	1	Warren, Batt	2	5
Tinker, William	4	2	Walsh, Walter	1	1
Tracey, Usher	1	1	Wing, Capt. Peter		
Todd, Thos. (Back Neck)			White, John	3	2
Tremble, Wm.	4	3	Wigley, Wm.	2	1
Todd, Joseph	2	3	Willson, Hugh	3	3
Turner, Charles	1	2	Willson, David	1	3
Tillyard, William	2	3	Waistcoate, Nicholas	4	2
Travis, Col.	4	5	Williams Richard	1	1
Tremble, John	1	1	Wingender, Peter	2	2

1783 TAX LIST OF BALTIMORE COUNTY, MARYLAND
Deptford Hundred

Owner	Male	Female	Owner	# White Male	Female
Williams, William	1	2	Wineman, Henry	1	2
Weatherby, William (single man)			Weatherby, Daniel		
Wells, George	6	5	Wells, George for Mr. Sewell of Phila.		
Worthington, Thomas (Rope Walk)			Young, John (Sec. Capt. Tibbet)		
Yem, John	3	3	Yoiser, Englehard		
Yellott, Jeremiah			Jacobs, Wm. of Zachariah		
Smith, Job			Zene, Simon	3	2

Gunpowder Upper Hundred

Owner	Tract Name	# Acres	Free Males	# White Inhabitant
Alexander, Mark	pt. Sute?	180		
Allen Hugh			2	4
Adams, William (P)			2	3
Allen, John			3	6
Allen, William	Land of Promise	125	3	7
Allender, Joshua	Arthurs Lot	72		
	Reserve	18	3	8
Amos, Benjamin	pt. Brooks Cross	7		
	Abrahams Pleasure	13		
Anderson, Dixson	Reaves Neck	50	2	4
Anderson, William			5	9
Asque, Dirrimple			4	8
Baggs, Ann (P)			1	2
Bailey, Sam? T.(Bachelor)	(Sec. was James Moore)			
Bain, John			1	6
Bain, William (Bachelor)				
Baker, Charles Sr.	Pork Forest	200		
	Hicks Adventure	100		
	Roless Adventure	52		
	Jacobs Lott	25		
	pt. Bonds Forest	42		
	Jamaica	22		
	Gays Timber Wood	30		
	Honesty's Best Policy	40		
	Hicks Addition	18	2	3
Baker, Charles Jr.	pt. Clarksons Hope	146	3	8
Baker, Charles of Lem'l.			2	5

1783 TAX LIST OF BALTIMORE COUNTY, MARYLAND
Gunpowder Upper Hundred

Owner	Tract Name	# Acres	Free Males	# White Inhabitants
Baker, Charles (son Lem'l)			4	6
Baker, Giles			3	5
Baker, James	pt. The Manor	168	2	8
Baker, John (Bachelor) Sec. was Lemuel Baker				
Baldwin, Silas	Judaths Delight	113	3	9
Baldwin, William	pt. Brooks Cross	5		
Banfill, William (Bachelor) Sec. was Jo Harritt				
Barnes, William (Bachelor) Sec. was James Rice				
Barrow, Elizabeth	not named	86	1	4
Barrow, John	not named	86	1	8
Barton, Asell			2	7
Benner, John (P)			2	3
Bishop, William			4	6
Bosley, Capt. James	pt. Hills Forest	431		
	pt. Hills Forest	200		
	pt. James Chance	80		
	pt. Who tho't it	140		
	pt. Gassaways	100	5	8
Bosley, James of Wm.	pt. Delaney	100		
Boucher, Thomas (P)			1	2
Bowen, Edward (P)			2	4
Boyce, Benjamin	Hutchins Lott	282		
Bradley, Edward (Bachelor)				
Bradley, Thomas			3	8
Bramley, William (P)			1	3
Brees, Luke			3	7
Brerton, Joseph			5	9
Britton, Richard	pt. Bathany Cambria	354		
Britton, Samuel			3	7
Brown, William			2	4
Bruthenton, Thomas (Bachelor) Sec. was James Bosley				
Buchanan, Capt. George-Hutchins Neglect		33 1/2		
	Quinn	500		
	Clarks Forest	540		
	Hills Camp	300		
Buck, Thomas (Bachelor) Sec. was Samuel Swarth				
Burgess, Henry (Bachelor)				
Burton, Thomas			3	4
Burton, William	not named	30	1	2
Bussey, Bennett	not named			
Bussey, Edward	Busseys Purchase	226	2	3
Bussey, Jesse, Esq.	pt. Hills Camp	450	3	7

1783 TAX LIST OF BALTIMORE COUNTY, MARYLAND
Gunpowder Upper Hundred

Owner	Tract Name	# Acres	Free Males	# White Inhabitants
Butler, Mary	pt. Gunpowder Manor	80		
Butler, Mary				1
Caley, Margaret	pt. Truemans Acquaintance	16		2
Camp, William (Bachelor) Sec. was Susannah Smith				
Cannady, John			4	9
Cannady, Thomas (P)			2	4
Carnan, Charles R.	pt. Taylors Pur'tis	530		
	Land of Promise	140		
Carter, Dinnis (P)			3	8
Cathcart, William (Bachelor) Sec. was Andrew Guiten				
Chamberlain, Elizabeth	pt. Gunpowder Manor	60	?	5
Chamberlain, James			1	5
Chamberlain, John	pt. Gunpowder Manor	240	1	5
Chamberlain, Philip	pt. Gunpowder Manor	130	3	10
Chamberlain, Thomas	pt. Gunpowder Manor	85	1	5
Chance, John	James Lot	62	2	3
Chandler, William			3	6
Cherry, Stephen			1	3
Chattle, Wm. (Bachelor) Sec. was Jo Hitton, Jr.				
Chears, John (P)			2	7
Clarke, Benjamin			2	4
Clay, Abraham			4	6
Clayton, Joseph			2	7
Colinas John			3	5
Combs, Coleman	Eph'm Say & Jo Thompson	107	6	9
Cook, James			5	7
Corbin, Abraham	pt. Dulaneys	200	4	7
Cord, Stephen			3	6
Cousins, George			4	7
Covenhover, Jacob (Sec. for John Covenhover)				
Covenhover, John (Bachelor) Sec. was Jacob Covenhover				
Cowing, William			2	5
Cox, John (Bachelor) Sec. was James Roney				
Crawner, Jacob			1	2
Cromwell, John	Wignals Rest	184		
	Fox Hall	50		
	Watertons Neglect	6 1/2		
	Owners Landing	16		
	Wibett	15	3	9
Croskey, Francis	Lawsons Farm	200	4	6
Crudgengton, George			4	8

1783 TAX LIST OF BALTIMORE COUNTY, MARYLAND
Gunpowder Upper Hundred

Owner	Tract Name	# Acres	Free Males	# White Inhabitants
Cromwell, Wm. Jr.	Coxs Fancy	100		
	Richardsons Neglect	57		
	Lucky Addition	15		
	Towsons Chance	18	1	4
Cullam, William	pt. Dulaney	120	7	9
Darnell, H. Bennett	Land of Promise	1000	1	1
Dean, Christopher	Wm. The Conqueror	277		
	pt. James Delight	37		2
Dear, Benjamin			2	5
Ditto, Abraham	Gads Delight	100		
	William's Refuge	20	1	3
Dimmitt, James	Demmitts Delight	80		
	Add. to Demmitts Delight	166 1/2		
	pt. My Ladys Manor	133	5	10
Dimmitt (Demitt) Wm.	Carters Rock	163	6	12
Ditto, Henry (Bachelor) Sec. Was Abraham Ditto				
Divers, Ananias	Swanson	66		
	Simms Chance	34		
Divers (Divas) Christopher			4	5
Dobbin, John (Bachelor)				
Donnevan John			3	6
Dorsey, Stephen (Bachelor) Sec. was John Cromwell				
Doughty, Patrick (Bachelor) Sec. was Patrick Flanagan				
Doughty, Thomas			3	6
Downs, Joseph (P)			4	5
Due, Robert			3	6
Dulany, Daniel			1	1
Duly, James (Bachelor) Sec. was William Sanders				
Eady, Jonathan			2	5
Earmin, Benjamin (Bachelor)				
Elliott, James	Elliott Risk	200	1	4
Elliott, James Jr.			5	9
Elliott, John	lease land	84	4	7
Elliott, Nicholas			3	5
Enloes, James			2	6
Enloes, John			2	4
Enloes, William (P)			3	7
Erwin, William (Bachelor)				
Evans, John			2	4
Everitt, William			5	8
Field, Robert (Bachelor) Sec. Charles Gorsuch				

1783 TAX LIST OF BALTIMORE COUNTY, MARYLAND
Gunpowder Upper Hundred

Owner	Tract Name	# Acres	Free Males	# White Inhabitants
Fielding, John (P)			1	2
Fitzhugh, George	Winsor	500		
	pt. Stute?	1000		
	pt. Delany	100	3	5
Fitzmorris, James (P)			3	6
Flanagan, Patrick (Bachelor) Sec. was Patrick Flanagan, Sr.				
Ford, James	pt. Gunpowder Manor	100	6	9
Ford, Ralph (P)			2	4
Foster, Abraham (P)			3	4
Fowler, Thomas			1	4
Fox, Richard (P)			3	5
Franklin, Benjamin			1	1
Franklin, James	pt. B. Manor	646		
Franklin, Major Thomas-pt. Dulaneys		106		
	F. Delight & Ruth Garden?	123	1	2
Franklin, Thomas Jr.			1	1
Frost, Jn'o (Bachelor) Sec. was Charles Baker				
Gad, Thomas (Bachelor) Sec. was William Gad				
Gad, William	pt. B. Manor			
Gallaway, Aquilla	pt. Dulaneys	50	5	8
Gardner, George (P)	3		3	6
Gardner, John (P)			4	7
Gittings, James Esq.	Gittings Choice	845		
	pt. Gunpowder Manor	237		
	Reserve	75	5	9
Gittings, James of Thos.	pt. Thompsons Choice	266 1/2-2		4
Gittings, Thomas	Thompsons Chance	533 1/2-5		6
Golding, Jn'o			4	8
Goldsmith, William C.			4	6
Goodwin, William	pt. Affinty & Abriteres (Aberilla's?)			
	Garden	500		
	pt. Suel (Sewell?)	180		
Gordon Charles			2	5
Gordon Charles (Bachelor) Sec. was William Gordon				
Gordon William	Honesty's Neighbors	80	1	1
Gorsuch, Charles of Chas.-Clarksons Hope		300	3	6
Gott, Jonathan (Bachelor) Sec. was Sutton Gudgeon				
Green, Clement	Brooks Cross	236	2	5
Green, George	pt. Burtons Land	11 1/2		
Green, George Jr.			4	9
Green, Thomas	pt. Gunpowder Manor	57 1/2-8		13
Young, Rebecca	Youngs Escape	1100		
	Sewells Fancy 750 a. & Nanjemy 375		3	8

-30-

1783 TAX LIST OF BALTIMORE COUNTY, MARYLAND
Gunpowder Upper Hundred

Owner	Tract Name	# Acres	Free Males	# White Inhabitants
Greenfield, Micajah			3	4
Greenfield, Pheby	Truemans Acquaintance	133	3	6
Greenfield, Thomas (Bachelor) Sec. was Philip Greenfield				
Greenfield, William (P)			1	2
Griffin, Andrew			3	6
Griffin, Samuel			2	5
Griffith, Philip	pt. Brooks Cross	384	6	14
Grover, John (Bachelor) Sec. was Wm. Grover				
Grover, William	pt. Delaneys	50	5	10
Gudgeon, Sutton	Dublin	100		
	Carrolls Adventure	116		
Guin, William	pt. Bonds Water Mills	40	5	11
Guiton, Benjamin	pt. Abrahams Pleasure &			
	Demitts Choice & #2	134	4	9
Guiton, Benjamin Jr.			1	2
Guiton, Henry	Come By Chance	200		
	Jamaica	120	6	10
Guiton, Underwood	pt. Demitts Chance	100		
	pt. Demitts Chance #2	18	6	11
Cuthery, Edward	Enloes Desire	42		
	Enloes Shift & Cutherys Chance-117		2	3
Hackley, John(P)			1	2
Hall, Francis	Land of Prommise	218		
Hall, Aquila Esq.	Tolleys Purchase	700		
	Taskers Camp(Note: Capt. Ridgely to pay)	200	2	5
Hall, James			4	6
Hall, Thomas			3	6
Hall, Hale? Wm.	pt. Bladesn M(anor?)		4	10
Hall, William Jr. (Bachelor) Sec. was William Hall				
Hanager, Patrick			3	6
Harrison, Thomas	Owners Landing	16		
(estate Of)	James Park	36		
Harritt, John	no name	100	2	4
Herritt, Richard			3	4
Hartley, Joseph			6	9
Hatton, Aquilla (P)			5	8
Headington, Abel	pt. Bladens	144	3	7
Headington, Elizabeth	pt. Bladens M(anor)	242	3	9
Headington, Zebulon			1	3
Hendon, Henry	Hendons Hope	40		
Hendon, Richard	Hendons Hope	40	1	1

1783 TAX LIST OF BALTIMORE COUNTY, MARYLAND
Gunpowder Upper Hundred

Owner	Tract Name	# Acres	Free Males	# White Inhabitants
Hill, Tower (nego)				
Hilton, James			1	1
Hilton, John			2	5
Hilton, John Jr.			1	2
Hilton, Joseph	pt. Gunpowder Manor	50	9	14
Hines, Samuel (P)			2	5
Holland, George (P)			3	5
Holland, John	pt. Bonds Forest	190	1	3
Holland, John Jr.			2	4
Holland, Samuel			3	8
Hooper Elizabeth (P)			0	2
Hooper, Isaac			3	4
Hooper, James			4	5
Hooper, John			3	11
Hooper, Thomas			2	5
Hopkins, Ezekiel	pt. Delaneys	100	1	2
Howard, John Beale	James Forest	125		
	pt. Annapolis	140	2	6
	pt. Richards Hope	200	2	6
Howard, Robert			4	6
Howard, Thomas G.	Cambridge	294		
	pt. Annapolis	10		
	pt. Pimlico	192	4	10
Hunt, James			2	4
Hunt, Simon	Youngs Escape	100	5	10
Hunter, George	pt. Gunpowder Manor	364	5	9
Hunter, Peter			4	8
Hutchins, Thomas	pt. Bladens	272		
Isgrig, William			4	7
Jackson, Abel (Bachelor) Sec. was Jonathan Eady				
Jackson, Thomas			1?	1?
James, John	pt. Standifords Chance	120	4	7
James, Walter				
James Watkins	pt. B. Manor	85	2	4
Jamison, Alexander			3	6
Jenkins, Ignatius	Land of Promise	425	3	5
Jenkins, Michael	Jenkins Purchase	288	5	9
Johnson, Robert (P)			1	2
Jones, John	pt. B. Manor	100	2	7
Jones, William (P)			1	4
Kidd, James				
Lagett, James			5	8
Howard, Capt. Jo.	James Forest	250		
	Leaves Chance 32-	63	1	4

1703 TAX LIST OF BALTIMORE COUNTY, MARYLAND
Gunpowder Upper Hundred

Owner	Tract Name	# Acres	Free Males	# White Inhabitants
Lagett, Joshua	B. Manor	70	3	8
Lagett, Sutton	B. Manor	70	3	8
Lattimore, John (P)			1	3
Laurence, William			1	4
Lee, David	pt. Cambridge	147		
Loney, Patrick (Bachelor) Sec. was George Rigby				
Lucas, George			3	5
Lucas, Thomas	Condem'd for a Mile	20		
	Thompsons Choice pt.	4	6	11
Ludley, John			6	10
Lynch, Anthony (P)			1	3
Lynch, Hugh Brady	no name	3	4	6
Lynch, William	Greens Improvement	18		
	Greens Park	64		
	Greens Neglect	100		
	no name	14 3/4	5	8
Lynch, Winifred	Winifreds Garden	120	2	5
McBroom, John (P)			2	3
McCann, John	Lynchs Desire	120	4	8
McCarty, Daniel (Bachelor) Sec. was Wm. Neel				
McClaslin, Elisha			4	4
McClaslin, Jacob	pt. Gunpowder Manor	250	3	5
McCubbin, John	Bollers Adventure	100	7	11
McCubbin, Samuel			2	4
McDannell, Martin (Bachelor) Sec. was George Fitzhugh				
McFall, Henry (Bachelor) Sec. was John Cromwell				
McGrill, Patrick	pt. Gunpowder Manor	214		
McLaughlin, Dennis			1	1
McSwaney, Jeremiah (P)			1	3
Magness, John (P)			1	2
Malone, Mary (P)			1	2
Marsh, John (Bachelor)				
Marsh, Joshua			1	1
Marsh, Thomas	no name	200	6	9
Millaman, Charles	pt. Gunpowder Manor	40	4	9
Miller, Hanah (P)			1	6
Moore, James	pt. Gunpowder Manor	150		
Moore John G. (Bachelor) Sec. was James Moore				
Morgan, Michael			2	5
Morgan, Michael (P)			2	5
Myers, Jacob (Bachelor) Sec. was George Fitzhugh				
Nash, John			7	12

1703 TAX LIST OF BALTIMORE COUNTY, MARYLAND
Gunpowder Upper Hundred

Owner	Tract Name	# Acres	Free Males	# White Inhabitants
Neal James (P)			1	4
Neel William	Browns Farm	279	1	1
Newberry, John (P)			2	3
Newton, George (P)			2	4
Nichols, Thomas Sr.			1	4
Nichols, Thomas			4	7
O'Brien, John (Bachelor) Sec. was Underwood Guiton				
Ogle, George				4
Onion, Hannah	name unknown	444		
Onion, Stephen	pt. Heathcotes Cottage	330		
	pt. Thompsons Choice	100		
	name unknown	150		
Onion, Thomas	pt. Heathcotes Cottage	320		
	pt. Thompsons Choice	100	5	6
Owings, David (Bachelor) Sec. was Daniel Rowen				
Parker, Edward	pt. Bladens Manor	26 1/2		
Pearce, John	no name	15		
Perdue, Walter	pt. Delaneys	100	1	3
Perry, Thomas (P)			1	2
Philips, Isaac			1	2
Philips, James				
Porter, James			1	2
Possen, William (P)			2	3
Rea, Benjamin (Bachelor) Sec. was Wm. Gwin				
Rea, Joseph			1	2
Reaves, Thomas			2	3
Reaves, William (P)			1	2
Reed, John (P)			1	1
Rice, James	Coles Manor	95	4	7
Richardson, James			3	6
Ridgely, Capt. Charles	no name	1064		
Rigby, George			1	2
Rigby, James (Bachelor) Sec. was James Gittings of Thomas				
Roads, John (Bachelor) Sec. was George Fitzhugh				
Roberts, Asel (Bachelor) Sec. was H.B. Darnel				
Roberts, Benjamin			3	7
Roberts, Benjamin Jr. (Bachelor) Sec. was B. Roberts Sr.				
Roberts, Richard (Bachelor) Sec. was Richard Howard				
Rogers, Benjamin	pt. Bladens Manor	193		
Roney, James	Lawsons Chance	100	4	6
Roney, John (P)			1	2
Rosenberry, Jo. (Bachelor) Sec. was William Goodwin				

1783 TAX LIST OF BALTIMORE COUNTY, MARYLAND
Gunpowder Upper Hundred

Owner	Tract Name	# Acres	Free Males	# White Inhabitants
Rowan, Daniel			2	4
Ryan, Thomas (Bachelor) Sec. was James Hilton				
Rion, William (Bachelor) Sec. was Jesse Bussey				
Sanders, William			3	4
Sanks, Zachariah			3	5
Sappington, Mark B.	pt. Annapolis	100	6	8
Sappington, Jo. (Bachelor) Sec. was M. B. Sappington				
Say, Ephraim - see Coleman Combs				
Scarf, John	pt. Brooks Cross	70	2	4
Scarf, Nicholas (Bachelor) Sec. was Jo Scarf				
Serjeant, William			3	4
Shaw, Robert			3	7
Shutter, Jo. (Bachelor) Sec. was Jo White				
Simms, James (Bachelor) Sec. was Abraham Ditto				
Simon, Mark (Bachelor)				
Slee, Joseph	Hills Forest	200	7	8
Sloan, Jo. Jr. (Bachelor) Sec. was J. Sloan, Sr.				
Sloan, Richard (Bachelor) Sec. was Jo McCann				
Smith, James				
Smith Jonathan (P)			2	8
Smith, Susanna	pt. Clarksons Hope	150	2	4
Snaler, Henry			1	3
Sellers, Jo. (Bachelor) Sec. was Dirrimple Asque				
Spear, Jacob			3	7
Spicer, James (P)			4	6
Sriver, Jacob (Bachelor) Sec. was Wm. Bain				
Standiford, Abraham			5	9
Standiford, David (P)			2	3
Stansbury, Dixon Jr.	Hills Camp	50		
	pt. Abrams Pleasure	25		
Stevens, Alexander (Bachelor) Sec. was James Baker				
Stewart, Ann (P)				2
Stewart, Elizabeth			2	4
Stewart, James (Bachelor) Sec. was Benjamin Guiton				
Stone, John			2	4
Strawbridge, Elizabeth			3	6
Strong, Jo. (P)			2	7
Sunderland, William (P)			3	5
Swan, Samuel			5	9
Swarth, Samuel			5	10
Taylor, John				
Theoble, Robert			3	4

1783 TAX LIST FOR BALTIMORE COUNTY, MARYLAND
Gunpowder Upper Hundred

Owner	Tract Name	# Acres	Free Males	# white Inhabitants
Wright Solomon			5	7
Thompson, Benjamin (Bachelor) Sec. was Simon Hunt				
Todd, Thomas	Gassaways Ridge	500		
Trapt, Robert			5	13
Tredwell, Daniel			2	4
Tuder, John			1	4
Tudor, Joshua			2	4
Tyson, Elisha	pt. Jo's Forrest	125		
	Bonds Water Mills	50		
Vennel, Richard (Bachelor) Sec. was James Gittings				
Warner, Edmund			2	4
Watkins, Samuel	Bachelor Hall	175	2	5
Wells, John			1	3
Wells, John (Bachelor)				
Westfield, William (P)			1	2
White, John	pt. Dulaney	100	2	5
Wells, Richard (Bachelor)				
Whitely, Thomas (Bachelor) Sec. was S. Gudgeon				
Wicks, Thomas (P)			2	6
Williams, Robert			1	3
Williams, Wm. (Bachelor) Sec. was John Hilton				
Wilson, Asel (Bachelor) Sec. was Major Franklin				
Wilson, Benjamin	Wilsons Discovery	31		
	Land of Promise	200 + 39 & 50-		
	Elizabeths Purchase	50		
	Wilsons Outlet	169	2	5
Wilson Henry			1	1
Wilson, John Sr.	pt. Dulaneys	138		
	El'h Purchase	40		
	Wilsons Adventure	90		
	Coxs Hope	30		
	S'o Addition	60	3	8
Wilson, John Jr.			1	5
Wilson, Samuel (P)			2	3
Wilson, Wm.				
Winslet, John			1	2
Witen, John			2	4
Wooden, Thomas (Bachelor) Sec. was S. Gudgeon				
Woolf, James	Greens Discovery	150		
	Abrelers Garden	50	4	6
Wright, Abraham	pt. My Ladies Manor	150	1	2
Wright, Abraham	pt. Gunpowder Manor	72 1/2	1	3
Young, George	Jamaica	50	3	8
York, James			2	4

1783 TAX LIST OF BALTIMORE COUNTY, MARYLAND
Middle River Lower Hundred

Owner	Tract Name	# Acres	Free Males	# White Inhabitants
Andrews, William heirs	Scotts Improvement	720		
	Richardsons Level	207		
	Swallow Fork	100		
	Violin	100		
	Cuckoldmakers Hll	50		
	Lye Sore	16		
	Rutledges Delight	50		
	Fullers Outlet	100		
	Ranging Forest	319		
	Bivens Adventure	156		
	pt. John's Habitation	100		
	Ebenezers Park	200		
	pt. Arthurs Choice	125		
	Batchelors Meadows	150		
	Ditto's Hope	300		
	Salt Petre Neck	100		
	Windles Rest	200		
	Andrews Care	50		
	Mulberry Point	200		
Durkins Adventure-50a. &	Alborough	324		
	pt. Daniels Town & Watters	100	3	5
Andrew, William			2	4
Arnold, Joshua			2	5
Alexander, Mark	pt. Carrolls Scrutiney	576		
	James Park	200		
Allender, William			4	7
Asher, Abraham	pt. Ashers Purchase	110	6	10
Abierism?, Robert	John's Habitation	200	4	6
All, Benjamin			5	7
Barton, Sillis			3	10
Bond, Thomas of Barnett	Bonds Care	500	6	9
Berry, Thomas			7	6 ?
Bond, James	pt. Bonds Neck	254		
	Andrews Neglect	35		
	pt. Limmerick	60		
	Nicholsons Discovery	69		
Bond, Luke heirs				
Brannan, James			3	8
Boles, George			3	6
Brown, William			5	9
Buck, Joshua			3	6
Bryan, James	Ravens Outlet	125		

1783 Tax List of Baltimore County, Maryland
Middle River Lower Hundred

Owner	Tract Name	# Acres	Free Male	# white Inhabitants
Bowley, Daniel	pt. Triangle Neck pt. Inloes Rest Resurveyed pt. Birelers Fancy, Dutch Neck, Low Lands & pt. Inloes Rest	382		
Britton, William			2	6
Bateman Henry			5	7
Bond, Elizabeth	pt. Bonds Neck	100	1	5?
Britton, Nicholas	Cub Hill	860		
	pt. Gays Inspection	150		
	Bartons Mount	16	3	4
Britton, Abraham	pt. Darnells Camp	236	7	9
Bond, Cassander				1
Buck, John	Golden Mine	100		
	Lukes Adventure	200	1	4
Briley, Thomas	Danby Hills	175		
Crook, James	pt. Black Woolf Neck & pt. Elks Range	200		
Chine, Elizabeth			1	1
Chine, Mary				1
Connoway, Michael			2	5
Cottrill, Sarah				1
Cartright, Abraham			2	5
Cole, Philip			5	7
Crumwell, John H.	name unknown	433		
Colvin, Philip			2	3
Carback, Mary			3	7
Coteney, Herculus	pt. Good Life	100		
Cowan, Alexander	Bear Nock	500		
	pt. Gays Inspection	50		
	Constable	50		
Carrol, Charles (Annapolis)	Thompsons Lott	300		
Carrol, Charles (Barrister)	Carrols Upland	398		
	Ashers Purchase	110		
	Long Upland	100		
	Hunting Ground	39		
Curl, William			3	7
Chase, Jeremiah	Oblong	150		
	Enloes Choice	150		
	Surplus land	33		
Dean, Manuel			4	9

1783 TAX LIST OF BALTIMORE COUNTY, MARYLAND
Middle River Lower Hundred

Owner	Tract Name	# Acres	Free Male	# White Inhabitants
Donton, William	pt. Casestones Choice	80	1	4
Delaney, Daniel			3	5
Davis, Ananias			4	6
Dorsey, Nicholas			5	9
Dunqin (Dunkin) Daniel			2	2
Donton, John			4	10
Davis Thomas	Authors Choice	45	2	4
Elder, Robert			2	5
Fell, Stephen			1	4
Felton, John			2	5
Fowler, Richard	Bachelors Ridge	100		
	Hinds Desire	15		
	pt. Sophias Garden Resurvey'd	133	7	3
Franch, Otho Sr.			4	7
Grover, George	pt. Daniels Town & Watters Town	80	4	7
Gallaway, William			2	3
Gallaway, John			2	4
Galloway, James	Gallaways Hope	257	1	4
Gallaway, Moses	Mary's Adventure	47		
	Fiddle Stick	50		
	pt. Gallaways Inlargement	308		
	pt. The Labysmith	18		
	pt. Arthurs Choice	40	2	3
Grimes, Rozin			3	8
Griffeth, John			2	4
Green, Edward			4	7
Griffen, John Sr.			6	10
Garritson, Job	James Park	100		
	Surplus land	71		
Griffen, John Jr.			1	5
Gossick, Elizabeth			1	2
Gough, Henry D.	Lingons Neck	1129		
	Venters Ad'n.	102	1	6
Hatton, Thomas, heirs	Caswells Venture	98		
Hatton, John	pt. Richardsons Prospect	40		
Hatton, Chaney	pt. Richardsons Prospect	50	6	10
Hims, William			3	5
Hampton, Thos. Gill	pt. Small Valley	.5	3	13
Hendrickson, James	Dukes Palace	70	1	4
Harrimon, James	pt. Harrimons Frolic	30	5	6
Hollin, Gabriel			2	6
Handon, Henry			1	3

-39-

1783 TAX LIST OF BALTIMORE COUNTY, MARYLAND
Middle River Lower Hundred

Owner	Tract Name	# Acres	Free Male	# White Inhabitants
Howard, Henry	name unknown	537		
Hollbrooks, Elizabeth			7	13
Hughes, John			4	6
Hughes, Mary & Cath.				2
Hart, Henry			1	3
Hendrickson, Ann			2	6
Hendrickson, Joseph	Thomas' Purchase resurvey	150	1	1
Hanson, James	Bivens Discovery	30		
	Priviledge	12	2	6
Jones, John	pt. Gays Inspection	80	2	5
Jones, Solomon	pt. Gays Inspection	100	1	3
Jones, Richard			4	5
Jermin, John	pt. Triangle Neck, pt. Inloes Rest & pt. Abirillers Fancy	100	2	6
Jennings, William			1	3
Jones, Jonas			4	6
Legge, Luke			5	8
Lux Darby	pt. Lukes Adventure	200		
Legge, Nathan			3	7
Lynch, Comfort			1	2
Legge, Benjamin			3	3
Lawder, Ann			3	5
Legget, George	Lott Nos.	200	2	8
Legge, John			2	3
Legge, Josias			2	5
Meads, Martha	Francis Choice	200	4	10
Manis, Charles			3	7
Mildews, Greenberry			2	5
Murray John (Collier)			5	11
Miles, Thomas	pt. Gays Inspection	175	3	5
Moore, Samuel			3	7
Mock, James			4	9
Marshel, John			1	2
May, Benjamin			2	3
Mohaney, Daniel			1	2
Mildews, Aquillow			4	6
Mullin, John	pt. Bonds Neck	75	4	8
Nicholson, Nathan	pt. Limmerick	40		
	pt. Nicholsons Discovery	11	3	5
Oliver, John			1	2
Young, John Telly	Tibs United Inheritance	550		
	pt. Lukes Adventure	30		

1783 TAX LIST OF BALTIMORE COUNTY, MARYLAND
Middle River Lower Hundred

Owner	Tract Name	# Acres	Free Males	# White Inhabitants
Owens, Caleb	Pt. Arthurs Choice	80		
Parks, John Sr.			4	7
Pearce, John			3	7
Parker, Thomas			4	7
Parks, Aquillow			5	9
Parks, John Jr.			3	8
Parks, Elijha			2	5
Perine, Simon	pt. Gays Inspection	100	3	5
Presbury, George G.	Surveyors Point	500		
	Chestnut Neck	203		
	Groses Outlet	79		
	Cimney Hill	54	3	7
Qua, John			1	5
Ridgely, Capt. Charles	A Lott with a Forge	2268		
	Other lotts unnamed	1422		
	Note: James Park containing 610 a. they say it belongs to the State			
	pt. Brothers Choice & pt. Nottingham	586	2	2
Raven (Ravin) Luke	Lukes Adventrue Resurveyed	190		
	Triangle Neck	100	4	8
Rummage, Susana			1	6
Rogers, Enos			4	8
Rock, Fiddle			3	6
Renner, Tobias			2	3
Reed, William			3	7
Reaves Josias			2	4
Ridecker, Jacob			1	2
Stansbury, Abraham	Richardson Plains	220	2	5
Sanders, John			3	6
Renner, Leonard			1	2
Stansbury, Benjamin	James Beginning	50		
	pt. Gays Inspection	60		
	pt. Small Valley	30		
Sutton, Joseph Sr.	Hunting Quarter	117		
	pt. Colle Stones Chance	100		
	pt. Gays Inspection	182		
	Naves Inspection	50		
	name unknown	51	6	
Still, Benjamin	Rosemonds Fancy	95	1	3
Seddon, James	Rights Forest	100	4	9
	Surplus land	7		

-41-

1783 TAX LIST OF BALTIMORE COUNTY, MARYLAND
Middle River Lower Hundred

Owner	Tract Name	# Acres	Free Males	# White Inhabitants
Skinner, John	Darnells Sylvania	500		
	pt. Venters Addition	51		
	pt. Michaels Chance	60	1	2
Seddon, Margaret				3
Spear, George			4	4
Stuart, Robert	Lott #22	150	3	5
Sullivan, William			3	7
Sinclair, Moses	pt. Bosleys Expectation	100		
	Tower Hill	80		
	pt. Lukes Adventure Resurveyed	61	2	5
Thomas John			2	5
Tolley, Walter	St. Georges	1228		
	Nothing Worth	125		
	Long Point	107		
	Cane is Altered	8	2	4
Taylor, James			4	7
Voice, Thomas			2	7
Wigley, Edward	Addition to Albrow	44	1	3
Wright, Abraham	pt. Good Hope	5	10	
Wright, William	pt. Jacobs Inheritance	___	5	8
Walley, William			3	5
Walter, Thomas			3	4
Willson, John			3	5
Walley, John	pt. Jame's Fore Cast,		3	5
	pt. Joseph's Privilege &			
	pt. Horn Point	30	3	5
Wollar, John			1	2
Wood, William			2	6
Walley, Basil			1	4
Wright, William			3	4
Ward, Edward			5	10
Walton, William	pt. Black Woolf Neck	75		
Wetherton, Samuel	Hard Lion	300		
	Presburey's Discovery	12		
	pt. Nicholsons Discovery	103		
	pt. Bonds Neck	108		
	pt. Darnells Camp	286		
Weston, John	Taylors Mount	250		
	Dixons Chance	300		
	Taylors Inlargement	110		
	Northing Worth	57		
	The Island	4		
	Long Point	47	4	7
Young, Henry			4	8

1783 TAX LIST OF BALTIMORE COUNTY, MARYLAND
Middle River Lower Hundred

A List of Paupers

Name	Free Males	# White Inhabitants	Name	Free Males	# White Inhabitants
Bennett, Wm.	1	2	Jones, John Davis	1	3
Bivens Rachel	3	6	Jerman, Philip	2	6
Chambers, Wm.	2	4	Miser, Hannah		2
Corbey, Wm.	1	2	May, Thomas	1	4
Collins, John	3	5	Parks, Elizabeth	2	5
Edward, John	4	7	Proctor, Deley	1	2
Green, Richard	1	2	Robby, Richard	1	4
Gray, James	1	2	Rutledge, Penolope	1	3
Hughes, Solomon	1	4	Sutton, Henry	2	5
Harbour, Thomas	3	4	Shires, Mary	2	5
Hawkins, James	3	6	Storey, Elizabeth		1
Hughes, Henry	1	5	Watkins, Mary	1	3
Hughes, Francis	1	2	Sucker, George	2	4
Jones, John	1	2	Saul, John	3	4
Jones, Thomas	1	3	Waters, Elizabeth		1

Single Men	Security	Single Men	Security
Edward Alls	Benjamin Alls	William Hughes	Henry Hughes
James Burches	Joseph Hendrickson	Simpkin Harrimon	John Skinner
Joseph Bivens	Aquilla Parks	John Jones	Henry D. Gough
Tower Bell	Henry D. Gough	Thomas Jermin Jr.	John Jermon Sr.
Peter Geo. Berry		Aquillow Legue	
John Anthony Cline	Nicholas Britton	John Miles	Thomas Miles
Thomas Collins	Mary Jones	Henry H. Martin	Henry D. Gough
Wm. Clarke	Henry D. Gough	George Presbury	
Samuel Fuller	Daniel Dimien	William Pines	
Handy Ervin		William Peckwood	John Griffin Sr.
Otho French Jr.	Otho French Sr.	Mordecai Rogers	Enos Rogers
Samuel Grover		Gabriel Still	Benjamin Still
Daniel Gossick	Elizabeth Gossick	John Tugood	H. D. Gough
Darias Flairs		John Warrington	
James Hughes	Henry Hughes	John Bivens	

1783 TAX LIST FOR BALTIMORE COUNTY, MARYLAND
Middlesex Hundred

Owner	Tract Name	# Acres	# Whites
Armstrong, Michael			7
Aster, Christian	Knavery Detected	3	
	pt. Tom's Choice	2	
Baltimore Company	Constitution Hills	780	
	Parishes Fear	120	
	Newton	200	
	Peace & Good Neighbor	350	
	Parris Range	700	
	Nicholsons Delight	100	
	Laburinth	1200	
	Bare Hills	175	
	Randalls Fancy	6	
	Quarry	100	
	Ivy Hills	54	
	Pimlico	800	
Barger, Deter	pt. Tom's Choice	2	
	pt. Coles Adventure	1	6
Barnett, Andrew	Wooley's Range	100	
	pt. Bond's Garrison	50	12
Baughman, Henry			7
Baxley, John	Rogers Enlargement	116	9
Beam, George	pt. Derbyshire	5	3
Bell, Eve			9
Bell, John			6
Bell, Richard			3
Bloomer, Francis			6
Blueford, William			4
Bond, Richard			2
Boone, John	pt. Neds & Wills Valleys & Hills	150	7
Boone, Mary			1
Boone, Susanna			1
Boone, Sarah	pt. Neds & Wills Valleys & Hills	150	2
Bowers, Daniel	pt. Coles Adventure	16	
Bowley & Lux			
Brooks, Humphrey	pt. Darbyshire	100	9
Brooks, James			3
Brown, John			
Buchanan, Eleanor	Auchentoroly	626	
Buchanan, William	pt. North Carolina	197	9
Buckingham, Thomas			
Busling, Thomas	Jacksons Chance	100	4
Barney, Benjamin	Benjamins Mill Lott	56	11
Hook, Josephus	pt. Coles Adventure	1	4

1783 TAX LIST FOR BALTIMORE COUNTY, MARYLAND
Middlesex Hundred

Owner	Tract Name	# Acres	# White Inhabitants
Butler, Alce			9
Cassady, Patrick			5
Carroll, Charles (heirs) pt. Letter Loney		780	
Clarke, Richard			3
Cockey, John	Blunder	135	
Cornthwaite, John (heirs) pt. Rogers Range		116	
Cowell, Robert			2
Cragg, Thomas			6
Crawford, Robert	Hope	200	5
Cromwell, Nathaniel			9
Croxall, Richard	Brothers Choice	185	
Deames, Frederick	pt. Coles Adventure	2	9
Dimmitt, John	pt. Coles Adventure	20	1
Dungan, Benjamin			7
Enders, Sarah	Merryman's Neighbors	25	10
Ensor, Joseph (heirs)	Ensigns Grove	380	
	Come by Chance	282	
Fite, Henry Jr.	Jones Farm	50	
	Milford Haven Enlarged	27	6
Franklin, James			1
Franklin, John	Hawkins Desire	100	1
Gardner, George			5
Gerritt, William			2
Griffith, Benjamin	Sweeds Folly	16	
Haile, Stephen	pt. Coles Adventure	83	9
Hall, Philip	Elizabeth's Diligence	55	
Hanson, Edward	pt. Salisbury Plains	60	2
Helms, Leonard	pt. Parishes Range	100	4
Helms, Mayberry Sr.	pt. Parishes Fear	150	3
Helms, Mayberry Jr.			6
Hennick, Christopher-pt. Coles Adventure		1	7
Hook, Dr. Jacob	pt. Coles Adventure	19	5
Hook, Jacob of Jos.	pt. Coles Adventure	2	9
Hook, Rudolf			7
Howard, Cornelius	pt. Lunns Lott	6	
Howard, Ruth	pt. Lunns Lott	236	
Jarvis, Mead			9
Johnson, Dr. Edward			4
Jarvis, Edward			2
Johnson, Rinaldo	Turkey Cock Hall	200	
Jones, Thomas	Galley Pot Level	433	
Knight, Jacob			2
Gardner, Michael			7

1783 TAX LIST OF BALTIMORE COUNTY, MARYLAND
Middlesex Hundred

Owner	Tract Name	# Acres	# White Inhabitants
Johnson, Thomas	Pleasant Green	97	
	Turners Hall	200	
	Logstons Addition	100	
	Jamaica(?) Man's Plague	132	
	Cooksons Content	7	
	Quebecs Addition	9	
	Angels Fortune	55	9
Kramer, Michael	Germany	9	
	pt. Angels Fortune	27	
	pt. Cooks Adventure	9	6
Laurence, Richard			1
Lawson, Alexander	Happy Be Lucky	126	
	Haphazard	300	
	Daniels Whimsey	100	.
Leaf, Jacob			8
Lewis, Henry	name unknown	40	3
Longley, Benjamin	pt. North Carolina	50	8
Love, Miles	pt. Parishes Range	100	
Lux, George	Chatsworth	917	
	Welshmans Venture	100	5
Lyon, William	pt. North Carolina	235	
McAlister, Joseph	pt. Derbyshire	144	4
McAlister, Robert	pt. Darbyshire	182	
McLelling, John	McLellings Adventure	117	
May, William			3
Merryman, Caleb			1
Merryman, John	pt. North Carolina	264	
Merryman, Samuel	Cromwells Chance	124	
	Sams Meadows	39	2
Minshire, John			6
Moore, William	pt. Todd Range	10	
Moore, William (heirs)	pt. Todd Range	10	
Morgan, David			3
Morrison, Hugh			7
Mummy, John			5
Myers, Jacob	pt. Coles Adventure	6	
Orme, Samuel	Providence	1	3
Orndorf, Conrad			5
Pluck, John	pt. Coles Adventure	2	6
Price, Amon	pt. Toms Choice	121	5
Puntany, Caleb	pt. Parishes Range	80	3
Puntany, Sarah	pt. Parishes Range	119	6

-46-

1783 TAX LIST OF BALTIMORE COUNTY, MARYLAND
Middlesex Hundred

Owner	Tract Name	# Acres	# White Inhabitants
Price, Marth'	Absoloms Meadows	8	
	pt. Cromwells Chance	98	
	Organs Forest	106	
	pt. Toms Choice	100	8
Reader, Michael	pt. Coles Adventure	30	5
Reed, John	pt. Bond's Garrison	50	5
Reiley, John	pt. Hopyard	33	
Richards, James (heirs)	pt. Spicers Inheritance	75	
Ridgely, Chas. Of John	Ridgely's Delight	350	
	Pay My Debts	550	
Ridgely, Capt. Charles	pt. Todd's Range	23	
Rigdon, William			
Ritter, Thomas			5
Rogers, Philip	Bonds Pleasant Hills	198	
Rusk, Richard	pt. Coles Adventure	6	
Rutter, Henry	Monk's Discovery	20	10
Rutledge, Zachariah (Pauper)			3
Rutter, Richard			3
Rutter, Thomas	Valiant Hazard	146	9
	Timber Ridge	100	
	pt. Salisbury Plains	20	
Sellman, Johnzee			2
Shepherd, Nathan			5
Shids, Richard			4
Smith, John (farmer)	pt. North Carolina	50	11
Smith, John (merchant)	Deer Park	333	4
Smith, Nicholas			9
Spicer, John			2
Spicer, Rebecca	pt. Spicers Inheritance	25	3
	Spicer's Stony Hills	87	
Starrett, John	pt. Parishes Range	195	
Stevenson, John Jr.			7
Stevenson, Mordecai	pt. Enlargement	95	
Stigar, Andrew	pt. Chatsworth	8	
Swingle, Michael	pt. Milford Haven	100	4
Taylor, John			7
Todd, Thomas			7
Towson, Ezekiel	pt. Deer Park	135	8
Tschudy, Martin	pt. Coles Adventure	12	
Van Bibber, Isaac	pt. Coles Adventure	100	
Virble?, Daniel			7
Young, Jacob	Young's Delight	50	
	pt. Hopyard	33	5

1783 TAX LIST OF BALTIMORE COUNTY, MARYLAND
Middlesex Hundred

Owner	Tract Name	# Acres	# White Inhabitants
Warren, Jacob	Cooksons Polygon	16	3
Welsh, Jacob	pt. Bonds Garrison	422	
Welsh, James	Traymore	185	7
Welsh, Robert	pt. Parrishes Range		
Wooding, Beal			4
Wooding, John	pt. Parrishes Range	100	5
Wooding, Solomon			3
Wooding, Stephen	pt. Parishes Range	200	8
Woolf, Michael			8
Wright, Joseph (Right) - Pauper			4
Young, Eleanor	pt. Hopyard	100	3
Young, Michael	pt. Hopyard	33	1

Single Men	Security	Single Men	Security
Baker, Henry	Jacob Young	Buchanan, Saml.	Wm. Buchanan
Barney, Hugh	Thomas Rutter	Corberth, Aaron	Richard Lawrence
Barney, Pearson	Benjamin Barney	Crosbley, Nicholas	John Baxley
Hooper, Jacob	Robert Cowell	Hubbard, Henry	Michael Gardner
Lee, Samuel	Wm. Rigdon	Lee, Thomas	Wm. Rigdon
Leonard, James	Richard Laurence*.	Miller, George	Nicholas Swingle
Miller, John	John Gardner	Miniken, Patrick	Michael Kramer
Mins, Philip	Thomas Rutter	Morrison, James	Thos. Buckingham
Neighbours, Joseph	Edward Hanson	Orndcrf, Jacob	Conrad Orndorf
Pluck, Andrew	John Pluck	Price, Joshua	Marth' Price
Rigdon, Wm.	John Boxley	Ritter, John	Thos. Ritter
Rutter, Solomon	Thomas Rutter	Rutter, Thomas	Michael Kramer
Sibre, Wm.	Michael Kramer	Swingle, John	Michael Swingle
Towson, William	Ezekiel Towson	Trimble, Jacob	Edward Hanson
Wooding, Solomon	John Wooding		

---------------- List of Paupers --------------------

Allen, Bartholomew	Allison, Matthew	Ambers, Stephen	Baddock Andrew
Baddock, James	Beam, Philip	Bennett, Jacob	Bennett, Thomas
Berry, Michael	Brodbent, Joseph	Bray, Joseph	Button, Anthony
Canady, Sarah	Crawford, Leonard	Darr, Christian	Defnist? Wm.
Duckart, Thos.	Ford, Thomas	Ford, Wm.	Harris, John
Jaffres, Richard	Laurence, James	Mason, Chas.	Moore, William
Morrison, Wm.	Nappett, Saml.	Nelson, Andrew	Nets, Good
Parrish, John	Perry, Mary	Philips, Wm.	Preston, Thomas
Redison, Ruth	Roach, John	Smith, Daniel	Smith, John
Spencer, John	Stewart, Robert	Swan, Samuel	Taylor, Thomas
Tobitt, James	Walker, Elizabeth	Wilson, Samuel	Woodhouse, John
			Hooper, Margaret

1783 TAX LIST OF BALTIMORE COUNTY, MARYLAND
Middle River Upper and Back River Upper Hundred

Owner	Tract Name	# Acres	# White Inhabitants
Amoss, James	name unknown	150	
Anderson, Daniel			6
Andrews, Rev. John			5
Anson, Philorias	pt. Harrisons Meadows	142	5
Ashman, John			2
Bagford, William			7
Belt, Richard	Williams Chance Leased	117	9
Beston, Joseph	name unknown	62 1/2	2
Binnex, Barney	Binnex's Chance	67	10
Blatchley, Thomas			5
Bond, Edward	pt. Middle Ridge	100	
	pt. Gists Search	50	
	Bond's Inheritance	60	6
Bond, John Jr. ?	pt. Bonds Industry	300	5
Bond, John, Jr.	pt. Bonds Industry	150	4
Bond, Nicodemus	pt. Gists Search & pt. Middle Ridge	215	8
Bond, Thomas	Stones Adventrue	300	
Bosley, Caleb	pt. Chas'. Policy & Long Valley	120	4
Bosley, Elizabeth			4
Bosley, Greenberry	pt. The Forecast	266	8
Bosley, John of Joshua	pt. Bettys Adventure	50	
	pt. Nicholas' Manor	45	
	pt. Add. to Taylors String	125	2
Bosley, Joshua	pt. Bettys Adventure	245	4
Bosley, Thomas	pt. Volcania	50	
Bosley, Walter			8
Bosley, William of Joseph	pt. Nicholsons Manor	150	5
Bosley, Wm. of Wm.			5
Bosley, Zebulon	pt. Chas.' Policy & Long Valley	150	6
Bowen, Benjamin	pt. Regulation	252 1/2	4
Bowen, Jehu	Youngs Neglect	75	
Bowen, Joshua	pt. Regulation	252 1/2	1
Bowen, Josias Jr.	pt. Samuels Hope	150	
	Morgans Delight	110	3
Bowen, Nathan	pt. Samuels Hope	100	5
Bowen, Solomon, Sr.	pt. Samuels Hope	225	10
Boyce, Roger	pt. Nicholsons Manor	413	
Bond, Mary			2

1783 TAX LIST OF BALTIMORE COUNTY, MARYLAND
Middle River Upper and Back River Upper Hundred

Owner	Tract Name	# Acres	# White Inhabitants
Boyd, John	The College	100	
Bradfield, James			5
Brooks, Charles	Hares Meadows	60	
	Hog Pen Hills	67	11
Bryant, Luke	pt. Cumberland	100	3
Buchanan, Andrew	Banks Delight	77	
	Kings Adventure	65	
	Add. to Kings Adventure	20	
	pt. Chavey Chase	133	
	Broads Chance	149	
	Buchanans Palace	750	6
Buchanan, Archibald	name unknown	1102	
Buchanan, Eleanor			
Burk, Michael			2
Burnham, John Sr.			8
Carnan, Charles	Green Spring Forest	747	3
Carnan, Robert North	Shawan Hunting Ground	380	5
Carroll, Charles, Barrister-	Coles Caves & Mill	2461	
Chenowith Francis			8
Chenowith, Richard	pt. Long Crandon in the Hill	200	
	Henry's Delight in A____s	20	5
Chilcoat, Humphrey			7
Clark, John			5
Clawey, John	Johns Dale	77	4
Cockey, Carcilla	Cockey-Chance	46	
	pt. Parkes Death?	120	4
Cockey, Edward	Cockeys Delight	177	
	Cockeys Lot	2 1/2	
	pt. Friendship	11 1/2	
	pt. Severn Refuse	9	5
Cockey, John	pt. Cockeys Trust	200	
	pt. Helmore	200	
	Cockeys Recovery	150	
	Helmores Add. pt.	76	10
Cockey, Thomas Sr.	pt. Selsed &		
	pt. Poor Jamaica Mans Plague	400	
	Young Richards	225	
	pt. Spring Garden	27	
	pt. Stansburys Plains	350	
	Melinda	400	
	Prospect	1000	
	Cockeys Delight	59	2

1783 TAX LIST OF BALTIMORE COUNTY, MARYLAND
Middle River Upper and Back River Upper Hundred

Owner	Tract Name	# Acres	# White Inhabitants
Cockey, Thomas Jr.	pt. Lands & pt. Add. to Poor Jamaica Mans Plague	150	1
Cockey, Thomas Dye	Anthonys Delight	75	
	Dyes Delight	100	
	Cows Hill	47	1
Coddo?, Jacob			2
Cole, Abraham Sr.	Abrahams Delight	121	
	Add to " "	43	8
Cole, Christopher	Christophers Lott	100	
	Mountain	33	6
Cole, Mary (Widow)	Coles Struggle	200	7
Cole, Mordecai of Thos.	pt. Prices Good Will	100	4
Cole, Philip	pt. Mantion	50	2
Cole, Samuel	pt. Martinton	40	
	pt. Add. to Martinton	100	
	Coles Good Luck Resurveyed	34	
	Britains Meadows	8	
	Samuels Addition	8	10
Cole, Sarah (widow)	Thomas' Choice	144	6
Cole, Thomas Jr.	pt. Prices Good Will	334	11
Cole, William of Britain Ridge			
	Coles Discovery	39	
	Young Mans Adventure	200	11
Colegate, John	pt. John & Thomas' Forest	314 1/4	3
Colegate, Richard	pt. John & Thomas' Forest	314 1/4	2
Cookson, Samuel	pt. Samuels Meadows	106	
Cooper, Thomas	pt. Nicholsons Manor	1	5
Corbin, Edward	pt. Cumberland	50	
	pt. Blathany Cambry	19	5
Corbin, John			7
Corbin, Vincent	pt. Cumberland	62 1/2	9
Cox, Abraham	name unknown	68 1/2	6
Cradock, Dr. John	pt. Nicholsons Manor	349	9
Cristoson, Robert			3
Cristoson, William			12
Cromwell, Ann (widow)	pt. Nicholsons Manor	294	7
Cromwell, Nathan	Joshuas Lot	500	
	pt. Nicholsons Manor	151	
	pt. Hookers Lasting Pasture	100	10
Cromwell, Thomas	pt. Shawan Hunting Ground	320	3
Cromwell, Stephen	Todds Forest	250	
	pt. Nicholsons Manor	44	10

1783 TAX LIST OF BALTIMORE COUNTY, MARYLAND
Middle River Upper and Back River Upper Hundred

Owner	Tract Name	# Acres	# White Inhabitants
Daughaday, John (Dawhoday)	Nights Addition	50	
	Taylors Direction	195	6
Daughaday, Richard	pt. Taylors Discovery	245	9
Davy, Alexander Woodrop	pt. Tiptons Puzzle	100	
	Water Oak Ridge	60	
Dixon, Thomas			5
Dodd, John	pt. Good Luck & pt. Add.	170	
	Round About Neighbors	61	4
Dulaney, Mary	name unknown	1200	
Dye, Thomas Cockey, Esq.	Taylors Hall	1022	
	pt. Longs Dale	375	
	pt. Thos. & John Cockeys Meadows-550		
	Jerrah	280	
	Wasons Farm	178 1/2	
	Penelope Dye & Thomas Cockey Dye's Addition	213	
	Broads Meadows	100	
	Wilmots Grange	8	
	pt. Lancaster	280	
	Leaf Land	33	
	Norfolk	80	1
Edwards, Henry			5
Edwards, Joseph			3
Ellinor, Frederick			11
Ensor, Abraham	Aletheas Lot	96	
	Broads Design	40	
	pt. Teags Plenty Ridge	67	
	Young Jacobs Chance	121	
	Mysers Care	36	
	pt. Olivers Lot	52	
	Buffoloe	50	
	More or Less Certificate	450	
Ensor Abraham, Jr.			3
Ensor, Eleanor	pt. Shawan Hunting Ground	340	
Ensor, Elizabeth	James' Prospect	92	
	Regulating Vineyard	33	
	pt. Spring Garden	50	2
Ensor, George	pt. Spring Garden	50	
	James & Robsons Delight	100	13
Ensor, William Sr.			7
Farrill, Hugh (cooper)			5

1783 TAX LIST OF BALTIMORE COUNTY, MARYLAND
Middle River Upper and Back River Upper Hundred

Owner	Tract Name	# Acres	Inhabitants # Whites
Fishpaugh, John	pt. Hopyard	116	8
Ford, John of Wm.	pt. Benjamins Beginning	64 1/4	6
Ford, Joshua	Fords Friendship	100	3
Ford, Ruhanna (widow)	pt. Gists Search	100	5
Ford Thomas Sr.	pt. Fords Choice	101	
	Bucks Purchase	100	5
Ford, Thomas of Stephen			5
Ford, Thomas Cockey Dye	pt. Benjamins Beginning	54 1/4	2
Fort, Samuel	pt. Friendship	100	
	Add. to "	26	8
Galloway, Aquilla	pt. Gays Inspection & pt. of Venture Not	150	
Gent, Thomas	pt. Sallys & Mollys Delight	100	3
Gilberthrop, Thomas			6
Gill, John Sr.	pt. Batsons Forest	250	2
Gill, John Jr.	pt. Nicholsons Manor	110	
	pt. Hickory Bottom	90	15
Gill, Stephen Sr.	pt. Batsons Forest	125	4
Gill, William			6
Gillesland, George			4
Gist, Thomas Jr.	pt. Nicholsons Manor	360	1
Gore, Jacob	pt. Murrays Plains	111	1
Gore, Michael, Sr.	pt. Murrays Plains	176	5
Gore, Michael, Jr.	pt. Murrays Plains	75	7
Gorsuch, Charles	Canaan	120	8
Gorsuch, Chas. of Chas.	Coles Search Amended	260	10
Gorsuch Chas. of John	pt. Coles Chance	85	
	Gorsuches Adventure	32	12
Gorsuch, John Sr.	pt. Coles Chance	250	
	Contrivance	170	
	Bought Dearer	31	
	Green land	88	3
Gorsuch, John Jr.			10
Gorsuch, John of Thos.	name unknown	436	2
Gorsuch, John of Wm.	pt. Matthews Meadows	40	7
Gorsuch, Loveless	pt. Friendship	120	9
Gorsuch Stephen			1
Gill or Gorsuch Stephen of John	pt. Prices Favor	115	
Gorsuch, Thos. of Chas.	name unknown	160 1/4	4
Gorsuch, Thos. of Wm.			2
Gorsuch, William	pt. Matthews Forest	70	
	Bite the Biter	22 1/2	5
Foster, John	pt. Inclosure	572 1/2	9
Frances, Samuel			7

1783 TAX LIST OF BALTIMORE COUNTY, MARYLAND
Middle River Upper and Back River Upper Hundred

Owner	Tract Name	# Acres	# White Inhabitants
Gott, Anthony	pt. Gunners Range	100	10
Gott, Richard Sr.	Add. to Gott's Hope	150	6
Gott, Samuel	pt. Gunners Range	350	5
Govane, James	Drumk Hasle	840	5
Green, Abraham			2
Green, Charles			7
Green, George			4
Green, Isaac	Cox's Prospect	100	9
Green, John of Robert	Susannah & Mary	100	
	Greens Safeguard	24	6
Griffith, Abraham	pt. Pleasants Prospect	50	
	Ivory Hill	19 1/2	10
Griffith, Nathan			
Hale, George Sr.	pt. Fellowship	100	
	pt. James Meadows	100	6
Hale, George Jr.	Traceys Park	60	11
Hale, Nicholas of Geo.	pt. Traceys Park	1	1
Hall, Edward of Joshua	pt. Taylors String	129 1/2	
	Smallwood	50	3
Hall, Joshua (heirs)	pt. Halls 1st Design	26	
(deceased)	pt. Taylors String	129 1/2	
	Smallwood	50	
	Add. to "	20	2
Hall, Joshua Jr.	pt. Taylors String & Discovery-140		8
Hall, Neal	Good Luck	25	
	pt. Forrest	139	
	Hales Adventure	11	7
Hall, Neal, Jr.	pt. Bosleys Policy	28	
	Panthers Level	17	2
Hall, Philip	pt. Todds Forecast	206	
Hall, Thomas	pt. Taylors String & Discovery-146		8
Hammond, George	Mountain	83 1/2	
	pt. Todds Forecast	45 1/2	7
Harrimon, George	pt. Cumberland	100	
	pt. Talbots Slavery	44	
	Harrimons Best Way	10	
	Lemmons Enlargement	14	
	Add. to " "	6	
	pt. Blathana Cambury	152	2
Hart, Joseph			9
Headington, Nicholas	pt. Blathany Cambray	73	2
Hooker, Benjamin	pt. Wheelers Chance	147 1/2	11
Hill, Samuel			5

-54-

1783 TAX LIST OF BALTIMORE COUNTY, MARYLAND
Middle River Upper and Back River Upper Hundred

Owner	Tract Name	# Acres	# White Inhabitants
Harvey, William	pt. Nicholsons Manor	112	
	pt. Prices Good Will	60	
	Bedetton?	15	
	Low Land	7 1/2	4
Hicks, Abraham	pt. Hicks Forest	100	
	pt. Hicks Folly	11	
	Williams Folly	40	
	Dead Mans Advent	14	
	Addition	10	3
Hicks, Jacob	pt. Hicks Forest	105	6
Holliday, John R.	Goshen	418	
	pt. Northampton	475	
	pt. Fords Choice	101	7
Hopkins, John	pt. Friends Discovery	160	7
Hopkins, Richard	pt. Friends Discovery	315	5
Hopkins, Sarah	pt. Friends Discovery	160	3
Hunt, Fenus	pt. Bells Discovery	115	
	pt. The Groves	162	3
Hunt, Job	Smith's Addition	137	
	pt. The Groves	166	
	pt. Lulset Othen	180	4
Hunt, Samuel Chew	pt. The Groves	116	
	pt. Sulset Othen	195	6
Hunter, William	pt. Taylors Discovery	110	8
Johnson, Samuel			2
Jones, Joshua	pt. Nicholsons Manor		8
Jones, Richard	pt. Nicholsons Manor	390 1/2	
	pt. Chevy Chase	64	7
Kelly, Ann	pt. Gists Search & Kellys Delight	20	
Kelly Prudence	pt. Gists Search & Kellys Delight	72	5
Kelly, Thomas	pt. Gists Search & Kellys Kellys Delight	124	
Ketchpot, John			2
King, William	Kings Evil	33	
	Add. to "	33	
	Chance	20	
	Leafe	40	5
Knight, William			2
Lemmon, Alexious	Lemmons Lot	132	
	Battle Ray	33	5

1783 TAX LIST OF BALTIMORE COUNTY, MARYLAND
Middle River Upper and Back River Upper Hundred

Owner	Tract Name	# Acres	# White Inhabitants
Lemmon, John	pt. Teags Pleasant Ridge	33 1/2	
	Lemmons Outlet	27 1/2	
	Poverty Parts Good Co'y	33	
	Lemmons Choice	33 1/2	
	Lemmons Patch	26	
	pt. Pavement	9 1/2	
	pt. Fat? Brussells?	48	4
Lemmon, Moses			4
Longley, David			6
Love, Dr. Thomas	Cromwells Chance &		
	Cromwells Addition	169	
	Sheredines Meadow	11	
	Add. to " "	11	
	Sheredines Addition	7	1
Lye, Robert			6
Lynch, James	Find Me Out	30	4
Lynch, William			4
Lynch, Wm. of Robert	pt. Stansburys Plains	346	4
Lyon, Dr. William	Lyons Den	400	
Lux, Darby	Tryangle	300	
	Ridgelys Fancy	131	
	Pearces Folly	19	8
Lux, William			
McCarty, Callahan			4
McCubbin, William	pt. Roberts Forest	250	
Maise, John			7
Male, John			4
Mallone, John	pt. James Prospect	91	10
Matthews, Oliver	pt. Nicholsons Manor	210	5
Matthews, Rachel	Prices Delight	100	
	pt. Olivers Lot	202	
	Rachels Prospect	50	6
Matthews, William	pt. Nicholsons Manor	150	
	Connellys Delight	25	
	pt. Marys Meadows	100	
Merryman, Benjamin	pt. The Inclosure	647 1/2	15
Merryman, Elijah	pt. Cromwells Chance &		
	Cromwells Addition	300	
	Hales Park	92	
	Certificate	58	7
Merryman, Nicholas	pt. Bacon Hall	636	
	Merrymans Delight	455	

1783 TAX LIST OF BALTIMORE COUNTY, MARYLAND
Middle River Upper and Back River Upper Hundred

Owner	Tract Name	# Acres	# Whites
Merryman, John	Harriford	854	
	Merrymans Mount	49	
	Hab Nab Enlarged	120	
	pt. Elizes Grove	43	9
Merryman, Micajah	Merrymans Delight	150	5
Merryman, Nicholas Jr.			4
Moale, John Esq.	Shawan Hunting Ground	290	
Moore, Ann	pt. Red Oak Ridge	44	
Moore, John	pt. Red Oak Ridge	50	6
Moore, Thomas			6
Motherly, Charles	Bring Me Home	115	
Nailer, John			10
Nicholson, Benjamin	pt. Welches Cradle	513	
	pt. Nicholsons Manor	25 1/2	7
Norris, Joseph	pt. Conclusion	100	6
Norwood, William			9
Ogden Amos	pt. Hookers Farm	100	
	Hookers Adventure	50	3
Orrick, John	pt. Cromwells Neck	344	
Owings, Edward	pt. John & Thos.' Forrest	350	
	pt. Colegate Dye Owings & Charlotta Dye Colegates Add.-40		5
Owings, John Cockey	pt. John & Thos. Forrest	466	9
Owen, Richard (blacksmith)			6
Owings, Samuel	pt. Green Spring Purch	464	
Owings, Urith (widow)	pt. Green Spring Punch	285	2
Paine, Reuben			5
Parks, David			12
Parks, William	pt. Parks Death Knott	171	4
Pearce, Philip G.	Pearces Security	4	6
Pearce, William	pt. Mollys Industry	9	
	Pearces Lot	5	2
Pennington, Daniel	pt. Dusty Miller & B'd's Add.	120	10
Perigoy, James			5
Peregoy, Joseph	Union	156	
	Cold Friday	44	
	Eleanors Lookout	49	9
Peregoy, William			5
Phillips, William			3
Philpot, Bryan	pt. Nicholsons Manor	405	
	Add. Bud?	600	
Pickett, William			5

1783 TAX LIST OF BALTIMORE COUNTY, MARYLAND
Middle River Upper and Back River Upper Hundred

Owner	Tract Name	# Acres	# White Inhabitants
Pindall, John Sr.	pt. Friendship	90	
	pt. Gists Search	73	
	Pindalls Search	7	8
Pindall, Philip			5
Pitts, John			4
Powell, Benjamin	Talbots Forest	284	
	pt. Mollys & Sallys Delight-108		7
Prian, William	pt. Good Luck	8 1/2	
Price, Benjamin	pt. Prices Delight & Bare Hills-130		7
Price, Benjamin of John	pt. Sopeticas? Town	289	6
Price, Mordecai of John	pt. Sopeticas? Town	289	
	pt. Marys Meadows	200	12
Price, Mordecai of M'o.	Prices Chance	300	
	Prices Enlargement	64	
	Samuels Meadows	189	10
Price, Samuel	Prices Outlet	100	
	Prices Enlargment	74	
	pt. Samuels Meadows	375	10
Price, Stephen	Long Look	10	
	pt. James Meadows	100	
	Long Track	150	
	Prices Good Luck	40	5
Price, William			7
Prosser, Charles	pt. John & Thos. Forest	200	3
Randall, William	pt. Cockeys Trust,		
	pt. Helmore & pt. Cockeys Folly	289	3
Ridgely, Capt. Charles	pt. North & Southampton	2200	
	Sheredines Search	200	
	Drunkards Hall	256	8
Ridgely, Capt. Charles (with Lux and Co.)	Furnace & Mine Bank	1375	
Ridgely, Capt. Charles	his forges-200 tons pig iron		
Ridgely, Charles of Wm.	pt. Sulsett	150	
Risteau, Abraham	Fellowship Resurveyed	494	2
Risteau, George	pt. Shawan Hunting Ground	340	
Rogers, Benjamin	Benjamins Hills & Valleys	523	7
Rowland, Thomas	pt. Long Valleys	95	
Sadler, Joseph			10
Sater, Charles	pt. Saters Addition	100	3
Sater, Henry	White Hall	50	
	pt. Saters Addition	150	8

1783 TAX LIST OF BALTIMORE COUNTY, MARYLAND
Middle River Upper and Back River Upper Hundred

Owner	Tract Name	# Acres	# White Inhabitants
Sater, Henry	White Hall	50	
	Pt. Saters Addition	150	8
Sater, Joseph	pt. Saters Addition	100	
	Egypt Enlarged	90	
Scarffe, George			5
Sedge, John			3
Scott, Abraham	pt. The Meadow	120	
	Regulation	60	9
Sharpe, John Jr.			5
Simmons, Belinda (widow)			6
Slaymaker, Capt. John	Simms Discovery	136	
Smith, Andrew	pt. Teags Pleasant Ridge	100	12
Smith, Joshua			2
Sollars, Benjamin			6
Stediford (Standiford?) Edward			4
Stansbury, Benjamin	pt. Gays Inspection	98	1
Stansbury, Caleb			5
Stansbury, Richardson Jr.	pt. Add.to Poor Jamaica Mans Plague	110	1
Stansbury, Samuel	pt. Long Island	80	
	Add. to Long Island	140	6
Stansbury, Solomon			5
Stansbury, Thomas Sr.	Gossicks Choice	190	
	Stansburys Good Luck	90	6
Stansbury, Thos. of John	pt. Strife	124	
	Carrs Lot	150	9
Stansbury, Wm. of John			6
Stansbury, Wm. of Thomas			2
Stevens, John			3
Stevens, Nathanial			2
Stevenson, Henry Sr.	pt. Add. to Fellowship	102	5
Stevenson, Henry of Edward	pt. Fellowship	100	11
Stevenson, Joshua	pt. Fellowship	100	2
Stevenson, Nicholas	pt. Add. to Fellowship	100	3
Stewart, John of B'r T'n (Baltimore Town?)	pt. Sutter Hill	510	
Stone, Capt. Wm.	pt. Hellmore	340	6
Strickland, Henry			3
Swaney, Morgan			3
Talbott, Benjamin			4
Talbott, Edward	Barretts Delight	200	
	Barretts Addition	190	3

1783 TAX LIST OF BALTIMORE COUNTY, MARYLAND
Middle River Upper and Back River Upper Hundred

Owner	Tract Name	# Acres	# Whites
Talbott, John	pt. Long Crandon on the Hill-50		
	Talbots Slavery	60	4
Talbot, Vincent			6
Tatley, Joseph			7
Taylor, Joseph	pt. The Forrest	139	
Thrash, George			4
Thomas, John Sr.	pt. Olivers Lot	100	5
Thompson, Thomas			7
Tipton, Aquila	pt. Tiptons Puzzle &		
	pt. Bonds Industry	83 1/2	7
Tipton, Joshua	pt. Josephs Forest &		
	pt. Williams Forest	83	1
Tipton, Luke	pt. Williams Puzzle &		
	pt. Josephs Favor	83	7
Tipton Mary (widow)	pt. Williams Beginning	20	3
Tipton, Nicholas	pt. Tiptons Puzzle &		
	Bonds Industry	83	4
Tipton, Samuel Sr.	pt. Cromwells Park	363	5
Tipton, Samuel Jr.			5
Tipton, Shadrack			4
Towson, Charles	pt. Vulcane	150	4
Towson, Ezekiel	pt. Gunners Range	75	
Towson, Jacob Tolley	pt. Merrymans Adventrue	89	
Tracey, Bazil			3
Tracey, Benjamin Sr.			9
Tracey, Benjamin Jr.			4
Trapnell, William Sr.			6
Trapnell, William Jr.			3
Trimble, Cornelius			2
Tudor, Thomas			7
Turner, Matthew			5
Turnpaugh, Christopher			4
Tye, George	pt. Broad Meadow	100	4
Vann, John			6
Vaughn, Gist	pt. Bachelors Choice	183	10
Walker, Joseph	Mashes Mistake	260	6
Walraft, Thomas			2
Wantland, Abraham			3
Wantland, James			7
Wantland, Thomas Sr.	pt. Dales & Valleys	100	
	Thomas Wantland	98	5
Warfield, Caleb			10
Taylor, Henry			4
Wilmott, Robert	pt. Jeopardy	132	2

1783 TAX LIST OF BALTIMORE COUNTY, MARYLAND
Middle River Upper and Back River Upper Hundred

Owner	Tract Name	# Acres	# White Inhabitants
Wate, Richard Noatation	"I know not"		6
Welsh, John			3
Welsh, William			5
Wheeler, Benj. of Benjamin	pt. Wheelers Chance	125	5
Wheeler, Benj. of Wm.	Certificate	27	
	Prices Kindness	191	5
Wheeler, Greenbury			4
Wheeler, John			2
Wheeler, Nathan	pt. Bachelors Neck	50	
	Wheelers Chance	50	
	Tiptons Addition	70	8
Wheeler, Solomon	Hookers Prosperity	100	11
Wheeler, Wm. of Benj.	pt. Sings Range	67	
	Add. to " "	88	
	Brooks Kindness	11	5
Wheeler, Willison	Hockers Ridge	100	4
Widerfield, Peter			6
Wilmott, Abarilla (widow)			5
Wilmott, John of John	Litchfield City	60	
	Wilmotts Wells	77	
	pt. Rachels Prospect	60	1
Wilmott, John of Robert	pt. Bachelors Prospect	309	
	pt. Jeopardy	7	6
Woolf, Michael			10
Woods, James			5
Worthington, John Tolley	pt. Longs Discovery & Welches Cradle	295 1/2	
	Others Neglect	4 1/2	1
Worthington, Samuel	pt. Welches Cradle & Long Discovery	1250 1/2	
	Worthingtons Bottom	9	
	Georges Improvement	30	
	Fair Dealing	36	
	Casebolts Delight	50	
	Murrays Plains	137 1/2	
	Baxtons Forest	62	
	Towsons Inheritance	100	
	Hills and Valleys	81	12
Worthington, William	Crosses Choice	144	
Wright, Joshua			6
Yane, John	pt. Harrisons Meadows	240	6
Young, John Tully	Little Muth	228	
	Tullys Beginnings	14	
	Tullys Addition	30	4

-61-

1783 TAX LIST OF BALTIMORE COUNTY, MARYLAND
Middle River Upper and Back River Upper Hundred

This is a list of paupers and the number of white inhabitants in the household.

Allwood, Richard-2	Barber, Daniel-4	Belleson, Henry-3	Boaring, Ezekiel-6
Allwood, William-2	Bonner, Michael-3	Brangen, Jno.-3	Brown, Wm.-2
Burnett, John-?	Caldwell, Thos.-6	Carey, Andrew-3	Casley, John-4
Chitham, Wm.-2	Cooper, Stephen-6	Corbin, Mary-2	Deaver, John-2
Fannett, Wm.-2	Fell, James-9	Ferrill, John-5	Flatt, Ann-1
Franklin, Thos.-4	Goodman, John-3	Goodwin, Prudence-4	Goare, Amos-4
Griffith, Owen-4	Harwood, Wm.-5	Hatherington, Saml-4	Herbert, Wm.-5
Hewitt, Rich'd-2	Hyott, Wm.-7	Isler, Thos.-7	Isor, Rich'd-3
James, Solomon-4	Johnson, Wm.-2	Jonus, John-3	Jones, Honour-3
Jones, Thos.-2	Kennaday, Martin-4	Lane, Ann-5	Lee, Michael-6
Link, Stephen-2	McBride, John-7	Madden, Pat'k-4	Masor, Michael-6
Merrham, Joseph-3	Migley, John-2 ?	Norman, John-3	Offell, John-4
Pollad, John-5	Popped, Morris-4 ?	Price, Wm.-2	Pycraft, John-3
Pye, James-3	Ragan, Timothy-4	Riddle, John-4	Roades, Christian-6
Rochester, Thos.-6	Rockhart Jno.-5	Rownan, Wm.-2	Rywood, Robert-4
Sawyer, Thos.-3	Shay, David-4	Smith, John-4	Sollars, John-4
Sollars, Thos.-3	Stites, John-3	Stone, Hercules-4	Sykes, Nathaniel-5
Towson, Thos.-6	Tracey, Edward-3	Tudor, Benj.-3	Walker, Christofer-2
Wheeler, Wm.-2	Winks, Mary-3	Winteringer, Barnet-11	Worrell, Wm.-5
			Worthington, Wm.-2

Single Men	Security	Single Men	Security
Egan, Patrick		Arnold, Richard	Henry Stevenson
Bared, John		Barns, John	
Bishop, William		Bowen, Benjamin	
Burnham, John		Bowen, Solomon	
Burgess, Edward at Ridgely's works		Chenowith, Arthur	
Burkhead Dr. Thos.		Chenowith, Thomas	
Cole, Wm. of Sal. ?or Baltimore		Coe, Mark	
Corderay, John	Benjamin Rogers	Cottman, Joseph	John Willmott
Cullison, Jesse of Eb'n		Day, William	
Drewit, William	John Tolley Young	Dun, Henry	
Eason, James		Edwards Benj.	Edwards, Joseph
Englan, Joseph	A. Griffith	Ensor, William Jr.	
Felton, Hugh at Ridgelys works		Goodchild, Saml.	Micajah Merryman
Goodhall, William		Goodwin, Loyd	William Randall
Gore, Abraham		Gorsuch, David of William	
Gorsuch, Norman		Gott, Edward	
Gott, Richard		Gott, Richard of Richard	
Green, Benjamin		Griffith, Joseph	
Hale, Abednego		Hale, Henry of George	
Hale, Joseph		Hale, William	

1783 TAX LIST OF BALTIMORE COUNTY, MARYLAND
Middle River Upper and Back River Upper Hundred

Single Men	Security	Single Men	Security
Hall, Amon	Henry Stevenson	Hall, Charles	
Harvey, John		Hewitt, John	George Harryman
Hoggers, William	Benj. Stansbury	Hooker, John	
Hopkins, Nicholas		Housely, Thomas, shoemaker	
Hynim, John		James, William	John Corbin
Johnson, Francis		Johnson, Timothy	Thos. Hall
Jonas, Jonas	Benj. Rogers	Lawrence, James	Micajah Merryman
Lemmon, Samuel		Lewis, Job	Benj. Nicholson
Lynch, Lawrence			

MINE RUN HUNDRED

Abraham, Thomas	Wm. Goodwin	Allen, Ezeriah	Josiah Sparks
Armstrong, Aquilla		Armstrong, Nehemiah	Geo. Armstrong
Armstrong, Wm.	Geo. Armstrong	Barks, Francis	Richard Rhodes
Brumagen, James		Claws, Mathias	Wm. Pearce
Cow, (Cox?) Nathan	Jo Bosley	Cunningham, Thos.	
Cristerson, Thos.	Jno. Cristerson	Dollenton, Michael	
Elliott, Arthur	James Elliott	Fields, Charles	Jo. Stevenson
Fox, Joseph		Freeman, Wm.	Jeremiah Talbot
Gilbert, Jo.		Gordon, Jno.	Robert McClung
Green, Jno.	Jo Richardson	Green, Mesheck	
Green, William		Gullivan, Thos.	Jo Norris
Gumins? Thos.	Wm. Goodwin	Harper, Joseph	
Harper, Stephen	Wm. Green	Hicks, Elihah	Isaac Hicks
Hughes, Horatio		Hicks, Richard	Isaac Hicks
Hughes, Samuel		Jones, Saml.	Thomas Jones
Lacey, Samuel	Danl. Richardson	Lytle, Thos.	George Lytle
Male, Samuel	Joseph Curtiss	Meredith, Benj.	Saml. Meredith
Miller, Jo.	Thos. Travis	Parker, Oring?	Ab'm. Rutledge Sr.
Parrish, Nicholas		Plant, James	Wm. Goodwin
Ridenger, John	Richard Rodes	Plant, Samuel	Greenbury Wiley
Rockhold, Charles	Joshua Hutchins	Sampson, Abraham	
Shepard, Nathan	Jo. Shepard Sr.	Talbott, Henry	Sophia Talbott
Shipley, Thomas		Shorter, Wm.	Cpt. Jo. Standiford
Tibbett, Walter	Benj. Rodgers, Esq.	Vaughn, Benjamin	
Vaughn, Joseph		Watson, Arch'd	William Watson
Watson, Jo.		Wiles, Jo.	Christopher Meekener
Wiley, Benjamin		Bosley, Charles	Elizabeth Bosley
Gorsuch, Charles of Benj.		James, Philip	Jacob Splitstones
Sutton, James	Capt. Jo. Talbott	Johnston, John	F. Sparks
Willson, James	Jo. Norris		

1783 TAX LIST OF BALTIMORE COUNTY, MARYLAND
Mine Run Hundred

Owner	Tract Name	# acres	# White Males	# White Inhabitants
Almoney, John	Allmoneys Meadows	400	6	9
Anderson, Abraham			6	9
Anderson, Benjamin	pt. Andersons Lott	155	4	9
Anderson, Benjamin, Jr. ?			1	1
Anderson, Joshua	Love and Unity	300	1	1
Anderson, Mary			0	2
Anderson, Thomas	Andersons Lot	150	4	6
Anderson, William	Elizabeth's Delight	74		
	Andersons Intention	37	1	2
Ansell, Benjamin	Ansells Lot	14 3/4	1	2
Armstrong, George			4	8
Armstrong, Solomon	Bucks Range	46		
	Fugates Folly	67 1/2	2	4
Ayres, Daniel			3	4
Ayres, Jeremiah	pt. Carrolls Manor	125	4	6
Ayres, Thomas			1	4
Bacon, John	Smiths Lot	2 3/4		
	Martins Lot	126		
	Add. to Martins Lot	6		
	pt. Bells Lot	7	4	8
Baker, Joseph	pt. Grovers Meadows	60	2	9
Bond, Charles	Jonathans Lot	263	3	6
Baxter, Samuel			5	10
Bond, Edward	The Spot	250	4	7
Bond, Thomas Jr.	name unknown	50		
Bosley, Elijah	pt. Bosleys Plains	200		
	pt. Ditto's Addition	23	2	7
Bosley, Elijah of (P?)			1	1
Bosley, Elizabeth	name unknown	310	1	3
Bosley, Ezekiel	Sallys Lot	71		
	pt. Bosleys Lot	105		
	Fruitful Meadows	296		
	Reeds	100	4	10
Bosley, James	Bosleys Lot	250	3	6
Bosley, John			5	8
Bosman, Edward	pt. Carrolls Manor	243	5	8
Brada, James			4	6
Buck, Benjamin	Bucks Outlet	213		
Buck, James				
Buck, William			4	6
Bull, Betsey Ann & Wm.			3	8
Bull, Jacob			1	1
Burk, Richard			1	4

-64-

1783 TAX LIST OF BALTIMORE COUNTY, MARYLAND
Mine Run Hundred

Owner	Tract Name	# Acres	# White Males	# White Inhabitants
Burk, Ulick	pt. Bladens Manor & Coxs Forest	230	7	9
Burns, Adam			4	6
Burns, Michael			2	4
Carman, Andrew			3	5
Cavenden, Hugh			1	5
Cox, Abraham	pt. My Lady's Manor	94		
Cox, William	pt. Carrolls	1000	3	6
Cristerson, John	Cristerson	132	4	9
Cunningham, Thomas				
Currier, William	Almoney's Wilderness	50		
	Stoney Bare	100	3	8
Curtis, Daniel	Armstrongs Lot	128	2	4
Curtis, Joseph			1	1
Daley, Jacob	Stoney Up and Down	220	4	8
Davison, Major James				
Dillon, Andrew	pt. Billings	50	6	7
Dimmitt, Jn'o.	Cox's _____ sell	150	3	7
Dimmonck, Jno			3	9
Dixon, John	Young Man's Choice	165	3	5
Edwards, Edward	Cloe	40	1	2
Elliott, George	Elliotts Lot	50	2?	4?
Elliott, James	Elliotts Lot	114	1	10
Elliott, Robert			2	3
Elliott, William	Chas. Chance	75	3	4
Enloes, Henry			5	10
Ensor, Thomas			3	7
Fenwick, Ignatius	Carrolls Manor	4555		
Ford, Mordecai	pt. Carrolls Manor	67	3	6
Foster, George			1	2
Freeland, Abias	pt. Ploughmans	400	6	13
Fugate, Martin	Perdue's Lot	168	1	1
Fuller, Nicholas	pt. Hutchins Addition	89	4	9
Galloway, William	pt. Richardsons Lot	120	3	8
Galloway, Thomas	pt. Richardsons Lot	174	3	5
Gibbs, Aaron			2	7
Gilbert, William	pt. Snakes Den	97	2	5
Gillingham, John			1	2
Gillis, Robert	Richardsons Meadows	80	4	9
Given, John	pt. Standifords Lot	120		
	pt. Standifords Lot	136	2	6
Goddard, William			5	9
Goodwin, Rachel	pt. Bells Lot	208	/	1

-65-

1783 TAX LIST OF BALTIMORE COUNTY, MARYLAND
Mine Run Hundred

Owner	Tract Name	# Acres	# White Males	# White Inhabitants
Goodwin, William	pt. Purchase	117		
	pt. Benjamins Lot	400	6	11
Gorsuch, Benjamin	pt. Carrolls Manor	175	6	11
Green, Abednego			1	2
Green, Isaac			3	5
Green, Shadrack	Green's Palace	50		
	Green's Patent	30	2	5
Grover, Benjamin	Forked Meadows	30		1
Grover, Josias	Chamberlain's Meadows	75		
	Green Springs	25		
	pt. Elizabeths Delight	30	4	9
Hall/Halt, Simon			2	6
Hendley, George			7	5
Hicks, Isaac	pt. Carrolls		3	7
Hicks, Stephen			3	7
Hoffman, Christopher	name unknown	35	4	9
Hughes, Aram				
Hughes, Benjamin	pt. Hughes Prospect	56	2	3
Hughes, James	pt. Hughes Lot	33 1/2		
	Hughes Addition	40 1/2	1	1
Hughes, Elijah	Hughes Lot	33 1/2		
	Hughes Addition	40 1/2	3	5
Hughes, John Jr.			3	5
Hughes, Thomas	pt. Hughes Prospect	56	4	8
Hunt, Thomas	Hunts Adventure	160	4	11
Hunter, Samuel	name unknown	58		
Hutchins, Nicholas Sr.	Hutchins Lot	100	3	7
Hutchins, Nicholas Jr.	Loftins Lott	83		
	Plunketts Lot	131	2	7
Hutchins, William			2	4
Hays, Abraham	Hays Choice	96	5	5
Johnson, David Sr.	Lightfoot	116	4	11
Johnson, Jacob	pt. Carroll's Manor	100	4	9
Johnson, Luke	Carrolls Manor	177	6	10
Johnson, Philip	name unknown	98	4	7
Johnston, Dr. Edward	Mount Joy	3210		
Johnston, William	Norris' Chance	150	3	6
Jones, Richard of Ant.	Jones Lot	164	3	8
Jones, Richard of Rich.	Jones Lot	125		
	Downes Lot	114	3	6
Jones, Richard, Jr.				1
Hays, James	Addition to Bells	97	5	12

1783 TAX LIST OF BALTIMORE COUNTY, MARYLAND
Mine Run Hundred

Owner	Tract Name	# Acres	# White Males	# White Inhabitants
Kelsey, William	pt. Carrolls Manor	150	3	11
Lawson, John	Lawsons Range	300	8	10
Leach, Benjamin	pt. Carrolls Manor	40	4	8
Lewis Joseph				
Lobeshess?, Dr. Jo			1	3
Love, Philip			1	1
Love, Robert Pitstow	pt. Carrolls	100	1	3
Lucas, William			3	5
Lux, Darby	pt. Taylors Purchase	555	1	1
Lytle, George	Sinclairs Chase?	55	5	9
Lytle, James	name unknown	15	1	1
McBoyle, James	Cooks End	100	1	3
McClung, Robert	name unknown	225	3	10
McGaw, Adam	pt. Richardson & pt. Davi___	150	2	3
McGaw, Samuel			4	10?
Marshall, Sarah	Carrolls Manor	100	1	3
Meekener, Christopher	Ellens Lot	120	2	8
Meredith Joshua & Thos.	Sparks Desire	250	2	2
Meredith, Samuel Sr.	Locks Lott	170	1	6
Meredith, Samuel			3	4
Merryman, Benjamin	name unknown	182		
Miller, Hugh			1	1
Miller, John	Saplin Ridge	90	2	5
Morris, Isaac	Maynors Chance	200	3	6
Morris, John	name unknown	50	2	5
Morris, Joseph	Graves End	150	1	1
Morris, Samuel	Brunts?	100	2	3
Morris, Samuel	Addition	100	2	6
Morton, George			1	1
Myers, George	Small Hope	25		
	Myers Wires	19		
	pt. Tiptons	4		
	Sampsons	51	1	2
Myers, Henry			1	1
Newley, Godfrey			1	3
Nicholson, Thomas				
Norris, Abraham			1	4
Norris, James?	Add. to Shepherds Range	68		
	Enlargement	50	6	10
Norris, Joseph Sr.	Norris' Wonder	122	1	1
Oldham, Capt. Edward	Meadows Lott	117	1	1

1783 TAX LIST OF BALTIMORE COUNTY, MARYLAND
Mine Run Hundred

Owner	Tract Name	# Acres	# White Males	# White Inhabitants
Norris, John	Norris' Neighbor	100		
	Norris' Enlargement	50		
	Norris' Adventure	50		
	Norris' Addition	100	2	9
Parker, John	Hutchins Addition	89	4	5
Parker, Robert	name unknown	150	4	6
Parrish, William Sr.	pt. Bladens Manor	170		
	pt. Executors Management	100	3	9
Parrish, William Jr.			3	5
Patterson, William			3	6
Pearce, Thomas	Abrahams Exception	100		
	Bonds Folly	20	3	7
Pearce, William	Thomas' Frolick	40	5	2
Perdue, Walter	Widows Lot	100	1	2
Pocock, Daniel			1	2
Pocock, James of Danl. or Samuel			2	3
Pocock, James	Bills Meadows	200	2	5
Pocock, John	pt. Carrolls Manor	100	8	12
Pocock, Joshua			1	2
Pool, John	pt. Carrolls Manor	145	3	8
Price Susan & Zachariah	Patent	70		
	pt. Carrolls	10	4	9
Price, Thomas	pt. Bladens Manor	100	2	2
Price, Veaze		116	3	10
Prine, William			3	5
Quarterman, John			3	4
Randle, Charles			2	4
Reed, Joseph	pt. Merediths Lot	90		
		42	2	4
Rhode, Richard	pt. Grimm Garden & Charles Chance	222	3	8
Richardson, Betsey				1
Richardson, Daniel	Days Lott	155	4	7
Richardson, Jeremiah				1
Richardson, John	pt. Carrolls	168	1	2
Richardson, Sarah				1
Richardson, Sophia	pt. Carrolls Manor	100	4	5
Richardson, Thomas			2	3
Richardson, Zacheus	Hills & Hollows	40	2	4
Ridgely, John	pt. Taylors Purchase	1000		
Rockhold, Asoll			1	6
Rockhold, Charles	Rubys Lot	67	6	8

1783 TAX LIST OF BALTIMORE COUNTY, MARYLAND
Mine Run Hundred

Owner	Tract Name	# Acres	# White Males	# White Inhabitants
Rockhold, Jacob	Rubys Lot	200	4	7
Royston, Benjamin	pt. Carrolls Manor	150	4	10
Royston, John	pt. Carrolls Manor	134		
Royston, Thomas	Shepherds Range & Shepherds Range Enlarged	170	3	5
Ruby, John			4	7
Rutledge, Abraham Sr.	pt. Carrolls Manor	200	4	7
Rutledge, Abraham Jr.	pt. Carrolls Manor		2	4
Rutledge, Abraham of Wm?	name unknown	50	4	7
Rutledge, Ephraim	Pococks Lot	100	4	9
Rutledge, Michael			5	7
Rutledge, Thomas	name unknown	200	3	5
Ryston, Abraham			1	4
Ryston, Abraham Jr.			1	1
Ryston, Cloe				1
Sampson, Emaa'l			2	3
Sampson, Isaac	Lawsons Project	93	1	4
Sampson, Richard	Prices Lott	195	4	10
Sampson, Richard of Isaac	Colletts Adventure	175		
	S___less Dry Mountain	60	1	3
Selman, Major Jon'n	Rockholds Lot	105		
Sharp, George			4	5
Sharp, John Sr.	Sharps Lot	202	3	4
Shaw, Daniel	Two Brothers	110		
	pt. My Ladys Manor	270	2	4
Shaw, Joshua			1	1
Shepperd, John Sr.	Shepperds Lott	269	3	9
Shepard, John Jr.	Andersons Retreat	55	3	5
Shipley, Benjamin	pt. Carrolls Manor	150	4	8
Shipley, Benjamin	Add. to Piney Grove	101	1	5
Shipley, Edward	pt. Piney Grove	50	1	1
Simms, James	pt. Piney Grove	70		
Sinkler, William	pt. Carrolls Manor	185		
	Frizzles, Choice	110	2	2
Sinkler, William Jr.	Elliotts Chance	100	1	1
Sinnerd, Abraham	Rockholds Folly	100		
Slade, Ezekiel	pt. Days Lot	20		
Slade, William Sr.	Williams Lot	110 1/2	2	5
Slade, William Jr.	Bethel	192	4	11
Smith, Hugh	pt. Millers Gift?	55	1	1
Smith, Robert	pt. Merediths Lot	40		
	pt. Merediths Second Lot	5		
	Millers Gift	56	3	8

-69-

1783 TAX LIST OF BALTIMORE COUNTY, MARYLAND
Mine Run Hundred

Owner	Tract Name	# Acres	# White Males	# White Inhabitants
Sparks, Frans	Horper Spring	230	2	4
Sparks, Josias	Standifords Lot	100	2	7
Splitstones, Jacob	Little Plat	108	4	5
Standiford, Jo. of Skelton	Worlds End	250	5	9
Standiford Jo. of Jo.	Franklins Beginning	90		
	pt. Nancys Ending	90	4	6
Standiford, Skelton Jr.	pt. Carrolls Manor	100	1	2
Standiford, Vincent	Fosters Garden	100	6	7
Stansbury, Dixon Sr.	pt. Stansburys Chance	215	1	3
Stansbury, Edmund	Woods Lot	80		
	Hudsons Lot	82		
	Rutledges Lot	50		
	Slades Lot	40	2	7
Stevens, Ephraim			3	9
Stevenson, John	pt. Carrolls Manor	125	3	4
Stewart, John Sr.	Ezekiels Lot	260	3	5
Stewart, John of James ?			2	5
Stewart, William				
Strobell, Zachariah	pt. Richardsons Lot	25		1
Sutton, Joseph Sr.	Standifords Preserve	136		
	Tigers Revenge	114		
	Meadows	58		
	Adams Outlet	53		
	Haws Nest Point	48	3	6
Sutton, Joseph Jr.			2	4
Swan, Edward			5	6
Talbott, Jeremiah			2	4
Talbot, John	Little Honesty	44		
	Little Honesty Improved	100	3	4
Talbot, Richard			1	1
Talbot Sophia	pt. Carrolls Manor	170		3
Tate, Miriam	Jacobs Delight	70		1
Tipton, Samuel				
Trapnel, Vincent	pt. Carrolls Manor	204	2	4
Travis, Thomas	pt. Carrolls Manor	145	3	9
Vashall ? Augustine	pt. Bells Lot	87	4	9
Vaughn, Gist	Mount Pleasant	55		
Wadlow, John			4	6
Wadlow, Samuel			1	4
Wadsworth, Thomas			4	9
Wantland, Thomas	name unknown	150	3	7

1783 TAX LIST OF BALTIMORE COUNTY, MARYLAND
Mine Run Hundred

Owner	Tract Name	# Acres	# White Males	# White Inhabitants
Watson, William	pt. Carrolls	1	3	
Watson, William Jr.		1	2	
Wheatman, George	Mark Red	30	4	8
Wheeler, Wason			1	2
Wiley, Benjamin	Luckes Lott	137	6	10
Wiley, Cassandra	pt. Carrolls Manor	57		1
Wiley, Cassandra Jr.				1
Wiley, Greenbury	pt. Carrolls Manor	113	2	5
Wiley, John			1	2
Wiley, Joshua			2	3
Wiley, Vincent	pt. Carrolls Manor	135	4	10
Wiley, Walter	Bonds Folly	637	1	6
Wiley, William	Wileys Lot	104	4	8
Williams, Thomas	Deer Park	60	4	8
Wilson, Gideon	Hutchins Chance	112	4	6
Wilson, Jane or Jone	Richardsons Meadows	80	3	7
Wright, Bloyce	pt. Carrolls Manor	170	1	1
Wright, Thomas			1	3

PAUPERS IN NORTH HUNDRED

Bell, Nathaniel	Clark, Joseph	Carr, Aquila	Cullins, Jon'n.
Caters, Henry	Dickey, David	Huddlestone, Robert	Hollings, Jesse
Maloney, Michael	Mason, Peter	Perego, Moses	Price, Persotia
Perkipile, Andrew			

NORTH HUNDRED

Single Men	Security	Single Men	Security
Alster, Wm.	Moses Collett	Caple, Benjamin	Robert Caple
Cullison, Shadrack	Jesse Cullison	Caple, Samuel	Robert Caple
Campbell, John	Jas. Campbell	Cox, Joseph	Thomas Cox
Ensor, William	Henry Stubbins	Francis, William	Danl. McComiskey
Francis, John	John Brown	Foster, Thomas	Henry Lamevert
Gill, Daniel	Jesse Hollings	Morgan, Nicholas	Thos. Morgan
Moore, Henry	Stophel Moore	Minkey, Antony	Philip Minkey
Patrick, Benjamin	Daniel Mince	Skipper, Charles	Wm. Stansbury
Perkipile, Andrew	Jacob Perkipile	Spindle, George	Jacob Spindle
Ulier, Andrew	Margaret Myers	Willson, Abraham	Joseph Stansbury
Welsh, James	Thos. Tipton	Wareham, John	Henry Wareham

1783 TAX LIST OF BALTIMORE COUNTY, MARYLAND
North Hundred

Owner	Tract Name	# Acres	# White Males	# White Inhabitants
Arnold, Edward			1	2
Almack, William			1	6
Alceroad, Nicholas	White Rocks	60	1	4
Arion, Christian	Hills & Dales	100		
	Powells Desire	50		
	Gotts Grove	50		
	Arions Prospect	40	1	8
Adlesperer, Francis	Two Bridges	60		
	pt. Calaforna	100	2	4
Adlesperer, John			1	2
Armagust, Christofer	Whiskey Bottle	72 1/4		
	Arions Folly	41		
	Spring Hills	34	2	12
Byron, John			1	8
Bull, William	not named	115	1	7
Baker, George	not named	80	1	4
Bond, Benjamin	Fraziers Delight	114		
	Chance	48		
	Bonds Hazard	40	1	4
Bond, Benjamin Jr.			1	2
Barret, Edward			1	1
Brown, John	not named	27	1	3
Bond, John			1	6
Bosley, Elijah	pt. Bacon Hall	200		
Bosman, Edward	not named	112	1	5
Boring, James			1	4
Bailey, Adam			1	7
Bossom, Charles	Bessons Plott	68	1	6
Busbey, John	Hookers Prospect	57		
	Good Luck	80	1	6
Busby or Bussey John Jr.	Busbys Plott	70		
	Busbys Chance	14		
	Certificate	59	1	7
Brooks, John			1	7
Bosley, Gideon	pt. Greens Desire	200	1	7
Bowen, Thomas	not named	175	1	2
Boring, Joshua	New Germany	133		
	Add. to New Germany	50	1	6
Boring, James Jr.			1	4
Boring, James	pt. Borings Range	144		
	pt. Chaneys Ramble	62 1/4	1	5
Boring, William			1	8

1783 TAX LIST OF BALTIMORE COUNTY, MARYLAND
North Hundred

Owner	Tract Name	# Acres	# White Males	# White Inhabitants
Boring, William	pt. Greens Desire	125	1	9
Bosley, Thomas	Fords Folly	150		
	_____ Chance	150	1	5
Ball, Peter	not named	70	2	4
Barney, Absolom	Piersons & Benjamins Beginning-150			
	Pleasant Meadows	22 1/4	1	6
Ball, William			1	4
Bull, John			1	6
Boes, John	Poor Mans Barrack	100		
	Shitovers Choice	25 1/2	1	6
Bailey, John			1	2
Boreing, John of Reuben	pt. Three Brothers	100	1	1
Boreing, Thomas	Borings Struggle	50	1	4
Beaver, John	Beavers 1st Bottom	270		
	Beavers Retirement	25		
	Beavers 2nd Bottom	35		
Britton, Nicholas	not named	300		
Baker, William	Hemps Mile	30		
Bareham, Frederick				
Cole, Thomas	Add. to Quartermans Chance	94		
of Western Run	Add. to Peggys Delight	49		
	Coles Desire	77		
	Quartermans Choice	51		
	Abrahams Choice	94		
	Peggys Delight	115		
Cole, Vincent			1	4
Cats, Michael	pt. Stoney Hollow	50	1	5
Cullison, Jeremiah			1	3
Carr, Joshua			1	8
Chilcoat, John Jr.	pt. Henrys Folly	47	1	7
Chilcoat, John	pt. Robinsons & James Delight	40	1	3
Chilcoat, Joshua			1	7
Carr, Thomas, bachelor	His security was John Parrish			
Caple, Robert	Stephens Chance	18 1/2?		
	Caples Pleasant Bottom	124		
	Day's Pleasant Bottom	71		
	Spring Lott	120		
	Caples Dilligence	50		
	Point Pleasant	71		
	Samuels Purchase	26	2	11
Cole, Ezekiel	Panthers Lodges	50	1	6

1783 TAX LIST OF BALTIMORE COUNTY, MARYLAND
North Hundred

Owner	Tract Name	# Acres	# White Males	# White Inhabitants
Cole, Mordecai	Painters Level	100		
	Christofers Habitation	50		
	Mordecais Folly	15		
	Pleasant Prospect	50		
	Mordecais Square	14		
	Hotes? Outlet Amended	18	1	10
Cole, Christofer	Panthers Hills	100		
	Pearces Defeat	48		
	Coles Mountains	34	1	1
Cullison, Jesse			1	10
Cole, Broad			1	5
Collett, Moses	pt. Bosleys Chance	42 1/2		
	pt. Addition to Bosleys Chance		1	6
Calder, James	Castle Calder	662		
	Ohio	171	1	6
Collet, Daniel	Mount Misery	33		
	Blue Mount	32 1/2	1	12
Cross, Rebecca	pt. Bosleys Chance	42 1/2		
	pt. Addition to Bosleys Chance	150		6
Chapman, William			1	9
Cox, Zebediah	pt. Coxes Farm	125	1	7
Cox, Jacob	pt. Coxes Farm	30		
	Coxs Pleasant Meadows	100		
	Merrymans Choice	88	1	7
Cox, Jacob Jr.	pt. Coxes Farm	100	1	5
Cox, El'jah	pt. Coxes Farm	100	1	1
Caltriter, John			1	5
Cullison, William	pt. Sportsmans Hall	36 1/2		
Cullins, Thomas			1	2
Campbell, James	Hilly Run	180		
	Stoney Ups & Downs	35		
	Hobsons Choice	5 1/2	2	10
Clouse, Matthias, bachelor, His security was Wm. Hoofman				
Cullins, Sarah	Thomas' Poor Spot	113		
	Archibalds Meadow	64	1	8
Cummins, Robert	Coles Frolic	55 1/2		
	Watkins Desire	82	1	2
Cross, Joseph			1	2
Cole, Abraham	Spring Lott	36 1/2		
	Abrahams Ridges	240	1	4
Cross, John of Solomon	pt. Buck Range	100	1	8
Cox, Thomas			1	6

1783 TAX LIST OF BALTIMORE COUNTY, MARYLAND
North Hundred

Owner	Tract Name	# Acres	# White Males	# White Inhabitants
Cole, John			1	2
Crohorn, Patrick			1	8
Carlinger, Conrad			1	7
Cross, Benjamin	unnamed	52	1	5
Cross, Israel	pt. Buck Range	50	1	5
Crumrine, Abraham	pt. Ipstone ?	125		
Caltriter, Davall	Heidleburgh	50		
	Nightstone	134	1	12
Catere, Stophel	Milover	190	2	9
Coutz, Michael	Wispau	150	2	10
Cross, Solomon	pt. Buck Range	80	1	4
Casloe, Peter	unnamed	50	1	8
Crotinger, Henry	Belfast	50		
	pt. Little Britain	10		
	Powells Discovery	45	1	8
Duffill, Robert			1	7
Doyl, Jonathan	Guindle Woul	34		
	pt. Stoney Hollow	31	1	7
Dunkin, Benjamin			1	7
Dunkin, Patrick	Pollygon	340	1	1
Downey, Thomas	pt. Stansburys Grove	116	1	9
Dunham, Lowis			1	6
Downey, Walter	pt. Stansburys Grove	50	1	5
Davis, William	unnamed	100	1	4
Davis, John Jr.	unnamed	100	1	7
Davis, John	Davis Chance	100	1	4
Dorsey, Elisha	Stoney Level	172		
	Mount Pleasant	72		
	Dorseys Plains	388		
	Coles Meadows	152	2	8
	Petersburgh	300		
	James Lott	35		
	Towsons Grove Resurveyed	367		
	Hog Island	60		
	Days Choice	5	1	8
Deeds, Michael	Fair Play	61	1	4
Ensor, Darby	pt. Regulated Vineyard	67	1	1
Edwards, John	Edwards Chance	80	1	5
Embler, Abraham	Long Hill	67	1	10
Fights, Ulrick	Ulricks Delight	95	1	7
Ford, Barney			1	2
Finder, Peter			1	6

1783 TAX LIST OF BALTIMORE COUNTY, MARYLAND
North Hundred

Owner	Tract Name	# Acres	# White Males	# White Inhabitants
Fauble, Peter	Cole Chapter	33		
	Cole Pitt	27		
	Foubles Lott	240		
	Peters Addition	27		
	Petersburgh	100		
	Stoney Ridge	54		
	Faubles Barren Hills	35 1/2		
	Faubles Garden	33 1/2		
	Certificate	500		
	Catherines Chance & Parrishes Lott	409	1	5
Frazier, John(Jr. ?)	pt. Addition to Borings Range	83	1	8
Fresh, Francis	not named	78		
Fauble, Melchor	pt. Sportsmans Hall	38 1/2		
Franklin, James	Spicers Deer Park	250		
	Willmots Retirement	100		
Ford, Mordecai	Fords Choice	157		
	Kirby's Range	270	1	4
Fisher, George	not named	50	1	6
Foreman, David	not named	100	1	6
Fair, Stophel	pt. Wallet	108 1/2	2	11
Feather, Philip	pt. 3 Brothers	42		
	pt. Powells Discovery	202	1	8
Feather, Adam	Esenburgh	15		
	pt. 3 Brothers	29		
	Contrivance	130	2	6
Goodfellow, William			1	4
Gall, Michael	Shrusbery	214	2	9
Gaine, William	not named	50	1	5
Garlets, Henry	Big Spring	30	1	8
Grogg, Jacob	Young Mans Delight	50	1	5
Green, Nicholas			1	7
Gill, Stephen	pt. Nicholsons Monument	100		
	Lease	90		
	Addition to Henrys Folly	50		
	Certificate	47		
	Lease	64	2	11
Gill, Edward	pt. Nicholsons Manor	133	1	5
Gill, Nicholas	pt. Nicholsons Manor	115	1	2
Gent, Thomas	not Named	131		
Gist, Col. Thomas	not named	411		
Harden, William	Prospect	34		
	Neglect	33 1/2	1	7

1783 TAX LIST OF BALTIMORE COUNTY, MARYLAND
North Hundred

Owner	Tract Name	# Acres	# White Males	# White Inhabitants
Hallcok, William			1	7
Hale, Thomas	Hales Advantage	53	2	5
Hare, John	Boot	43		
	Jacobs Fancy	43		
	Add. to Panthers Level	15 3/4		
	Long Slipe	14		
	Good Luck	27	1	6
Hale, Henry			1	6
Hartman, Francis			1	8
Hicks, Nehemiah			1	4
Hicks, Isaac			1	6
Hicks, John			1	7
Hair, Jacob	not named	50	1	4
Hair, Philip	not named	50	1	4
Hurst, Bennett	Hursts Hills	400		
	Crosses Park	50	1	10
Hurst, Benedict	not named	80	1	8
Hosiel, Jesse			1	4
Hawkins, Thomas			1	10
Hair, Stophel	pt. Stansburys Grove	213	1	7
Hoofman, William	Paper Mills with mills	229		
	Barren Hills	15		
	Springfield	134		
	Christeen Creek	122 1/2		
	Eve	63	1	11
Horrick, Alias	Heidleburgh	160	1	4
Jordan, Thomas			1	4
Johnson, Jeremiah	pt. Elledges Farm	200		
	Nicholsons Manor	243	2	14
Kennedy, Samuel			1	8
Kittinger, John	pt. Shillings Folly	150		
	Scheming Defeated	39		
	pt. Shillings Folly	31		
	Kitingers Orchard	9		
	Kitingers Glade	24	1	3
Kittinger, Henry			1	4
Kailer, Jacob			1	3
Keeth, John	not named	30	1	4
Kidd, Joshua	Kidds Wilderness	61		
	Add. to Kidds Wilderness	35	1	4
Kalebough, Christian			1	3
Kerkehiser, Leon			1	4
Keith, William			1	5

1783 TAX LIST OF BALTIMORE COUNTY, MARYLAND
North Hundred

Owner	Tract Name	# Acres	# White Males	# White Inhabitants
Long, Henry			1	2
Lovedon, Thomas			1	4
Lemmon, Alexis	Johns Adventure	60	1	9
Lamwert, Henry	Little Rock	41		
	Middle of the World	77		
	Rome	38		
	pt. Plymouth	140	1	7
Long, Conrad	pt. Calafornia	135	1	8
Lemmon, Joshua			1	2
Lemmon, Jacob & Robt.	Springfield	511	2	10
Malone, William	pt. Robinsons & James' Delight	25	1	7
Matthews, William	New Hills & Dales	255	2	8
Maloney, Dennis			1	5
Mernam, John			1	3
Mince, Daniel			1	10
Marsh, Sarah			1	6
Medlicote, Samuel	pt. Quarterman's Choice	43	1	4
Martin, Charles			1	8
Morgan, John			1	3
Morgan, Thomas			1	3
Morgan, Mary	not named	22	1	4
Miller, Thomas	Coles Prospect	125	1	8
Miller, John	not named	45	1	3
Murray, John	Turkey Point	25		
	Pleasant Meadows	30		
	Add. to Pleasant Meadows	18		
	pt. Murrays Grotto	77	1	9
Murray, Wheeler	pt. Turkey Point	75		
	Murrays Chance	62 1/2	1	8
Myers, Laurence	not named	50	1	7
Moore, Stophel	pt. Calafornia	150	1	8
Myers, Margaret	Borings Meadows	153 1/2		3
Merryman, William	Merrymans Beginnings	50		
	Corn Hill	60		
	Add. to Merrymans Beginnings	50	2	8
Merryman, George	Merrymans Desire	27		
	Add. to " "	33		
	Merrymans Neck	65	1	12
Moore, George			1	3
Markey, Samuel			1	1
Matthews, William of Fork	Matthews Invention	53	1	3
Marshal, Jacob	Crosses Grove	70		
	Benjamins Choice	80	1	4
Matthews, Edward			1	4

1783 TAX LIST OF BALTIMORE COUNTY, MARYLAND
North Hundred

Owner	Tract Name	# Acres	# White Males	# White Inhabitants
Merryman, Benjamin	not named	168		
Merryman, John Esq.	not named	400		
Markey, Jacob	not named	55	1	4
Marshall, Thomas	Marshalls Folly	200		
	Sampsons Folly	118	1	8
Marshal, William	Rum	140	1	4
Marshal, Abraham			1	6
Miller, Peter	Overprone	24	1	4
Minkey, Philip	pt. Ipstone	200	1	9
Mortar, Jacob	not named	110	1	5
McComiskey, Daniel	McComiskeys Habitation	474	1	5
McComiskey, John			1	4
Matthews, Rachel	Matthews Forrest	400		
Null, Anthony	Nottings Lot	66		
	Add. to Nottings Lot	25		
	Anthonys Hope	24		
	Join All	10	1	7
Nailer, Samuel			1	4
Norwood, Philip			1	4
Nailer, John	pt. Greens Desire	25		
Owings, John			1	8
Owen, William			1	3
Orrick, John	pt. Bacon Hall	200		
Owen, Thomas	Hog Island	60	1	5
Peters, Jacob			1	6
Parrish, John of Edward			1	6
Parrish, John	pt. Prices Hunting Ground	55		
	Millers Meadows	38	1	6
Parrish, Aquila			1	1
Poe, Edward	not named	100	1	5
Poe, Edward Jr.			1	5
Price, David			1	8
Peddicort, Dorsey			1	5
Perego, Henry	Henrys Chance	235	1	6
Perego, John			1	2
Price, Milley	not named	70	1	5
Price, Thomas	Beavers Range	100	1	3
Bublets?-Rublets? Chas.	not named	100	2	12
Peters, George			1	6
Perkipile, Jacob	pt. Stansburys Grove	65	1	4
Perkipile, William	Coles Meadows	70		
	Stoney Spring	20	1	7
Petra, Philip			1	5
Pitts, Lewis			1	7

1783 TAX LIST OF BALTIMORE COUNTY, MARYLAND
North Hundred

Owner	Tract Name	# Acres	# White Males	# White Inhabitants
Rogers, Benjamin, Esq.	Pitt	1610		
Rawlings, Richard			1	1
Riston, John	Ristons Folly	53		
	Certificate	70	1	4
Ruby, Thomas			1	9
Rice, John			1	5
Roberts, John	Novascotia	15	1	9
Rinehart, Abraham			1	5
Roop, Martin	Add. to Michaels Beginning	57		
Ridgely, Charles, Esq.	pt. Troy, Georges, Etc.	900		
Randal, Thomas	Littocks Folly	193	1	4
Shaul, Joseph	Buck Ridge	85	1	3
Shaul, Joseph, Jr.	Stuckett	50		
Stoddart, David	Wm's. Struggle	135		
	Noons Delight	68		
	Small Hope	60		
	Noons Pleasant Meadows	37		
	not named	240	1	5
Stiner, Jacob				
Stubbin, Henry			1	4
Smith, Charles			1	4
Stansbury, Joseph	New Land Mark	91	1	8
Stansbury, William	Henrys Meadows	27		
	pt. Pleasant Hills	142		
	Certificate	366		
Skipper, James			1	5
Spindle, Jacob	Candle	268		
	Jacobs Desighn	70 1/2		
	Greens Fancy	69	1	7
Shilling, William			1	5
Shaver, William	not named	166	1	8
Shilling, Christian			1	4
Shawl, John	Jacobs Garden	20		
	Ammons Forrest	70		
Shaver, Christian	Piney Hills	180	1	9
Shangles, John	Stoney Bottom	80		
Singrey, Christian	Singerys Trouting Streams	178		
	Stevensons Hurtleberry Hills	100		
	Singerys Chance	153	1	10
Sullivan, John			1	5
Stelce, Philip	Coxes Park	80		
	Marys Delight	100	1	12
Stinebaugh, Adam			1	5

1783 TAX LIST OF BALTIMORE COUNTY, MARYLAND
North Hundred

Owner	Tract Name	# Acres	# White Males	# White Inhabitants
Stansbury, Edmund	Archibalds Level	48 1/4		
	Round About Flat Top	35		
	Talbotts Lot	64 1/2		
	Prices Chance	70	1	12
Smith, Thomas	Adam	77	1	4
Stansbury, Thomas	pt. Stansburys Grove	360		
	pt. Stoney Hills	900		
Stansbury, Thomas Jr.	pt. Stansburys Grove	124		
	pt. Stoney Hills	319	1	5
Stansbury, Charles	not named	300		
Stonebrinckner, Boston	Spring Run	117		
Sap, Francis	Prusia	50		
	Prium	36	1	4
Stiger, Andrew	pt. of Troy	715		
Sauble, Leonard	Johnsburgh	100		
	Pomerania	50	1	9
Shareman, John	Little Brittain	220	1	6
Stevenson, Edward	not named	150		
Tipton, Samuel			1	8
Tipton, Gerrard	pt. Borings Range	268		
	pt. Fosters Hunting Ground	294	1	1
Tipton, Thomas			1	5
Tipton, Jonathan	Coles Bottom	120		
	Brattens ? Beginning	12 1/2		
	Discovery	26 1/2	1	9
Tipton, Bryan			1	7
Tracey, Bazil	Traceys Hazard	84		
	Bazils Prospect	30 1/2	1	10
Tracey, John	not named	34	1	11
Tracey, Tego			1	9
Tracey, Warnell			1	5
Vaughan, Christopher	Vaughans Inclosure	22		
	Vaughans Parade	30		
	Shillings Pleasure	25		
	Spring Garden	141	1	10
Woodcock, Robert	Robinsons & James' Delight	86	1	5
Wolf, Jacob	not named	15	1	7
Wisner, Mathias	Wisners Prospect	360		
	Head & Tail	48		
	Stevens Addition	30		
	Stevens Folly	22	1	7
Wheeler, Mordacai			1	2

-81-

1783 TAX LIST OF BALTIMORE COUNTY, MARYLAND
North Hundred

Owner	Tract Name	# Acres	# White Males	# White Inhabitants
Wareham, Henry	pt. Borings Range	125		
	pt. New Germany	45	1	9
Wyman, Barnett	pt. Calafornia	100	1	8
Wheeler, Benjamin	Shillings Meadows	40		
	Add. to Barneys Ridge	50		
	Wheelers Enlargement	50		
	Elijahs Lott	50		
	Wheelers Purchase	50		
	Barneys Ridge	100		
Wheeler, William	not named	127	1	6
Wheeler, Greenbury	not named	50	1	3
Warwick, William			1	4
Watkin, Samuel				
Woodford, Frederick	not named	50	1	6
Walker, George	not named	179	1	5
Walker, Joseph	not named	100	1	4
Waggoner, Henry	not named	50	1	3
Wily, Abel	Marys Delight	100	1	6
Winks, Peter			1	3
Wagoner, Henry	not named	50	1	5
Wheeler, Benjamin of John			1	2
Wentz, Adam	Stumps Lott	22 1/2		
	pt. Smithfield	132	1	5
Willson, James			1	5

PATAPSCO LOWER HUNDRED

Owner	Tract Name	# Acres	# White Inhabitants
Armitage, John			6
Armstrong, John	name unknown	294	5
Arnold, Peter			9
Bowen John			4
Bond, Col. Thomas of Thos. -of Harford Co. -owned an unnamed, unknown quanity of land			
Bryan, James	Bryans Chance	50	
	Wheelers Lot	50	
	Bryans Meadows	110	
	pt. Hannahs Lot	40	12
Bowen, Edward	Causil? Resurveyed	246	2
Button, William			6
Bowen, Sarah	name unknown	196	7
Baxter, Joseph			8

-82-

1783 TAX LIST OF BALTIMORE COUNTY, MARYLAND
Patapsco Lower Hundred

Owner	Tract Name	# Acres	# White Inhabitants
Bowen, Josias	name unknown	408	3
Brock, Rachel	Samuels Lot	8	5
Bowen, Absolom			8
Buchanan, Archibald	name unknown	1270	
Baltimore Company	name unknown	3457	
Batty, Ferdinando	name unknown	81	6
Burling, Thomas	pt. Hails Folly	33	
Cole, Nathan	Stony Ridge	125	2
Carter, Ann			4
Cole, Thomas			3
Carter, William			5
Colegate, Thomas	Powells Point	70	
	Ruxtons Range	100	
	pt. Colegates Point & Colegates Last Shift	130	8
Cross, John A.			9
Childs, George			4
Chamier, Agnes	name unknown	834	
Cox, Mary		223	
Cunningham, Michael			3
Croxall, Richard	Hopesons (Hobsons?) Choice	100	
Davis, Cath'l.			5
Davis, Christian			5
Deaver, John	name unknown	125	
Duhurst, James			8
Deal, Henry	pt. Salisbury Plains	3	7
Davis, Daniel	Corbins Rest	50	
Donnalson, Joseph	name unknown	128	
Evans, Daniel	Fox Hall	140	9
Eaglestone, Jonathan			8
Eaglestone, Abraham	name unknown	420	7
Ensor, John			7
Ensor, Abraham	Darley Hall	300	
	Sea Ticks Plenty	314	
	Ensors Inspection	17	7
Edwards, Elizabeth	Burm's Forrest	48	2
Ensor, Joseph's heirs	name unknown	110	
Gorsuch, John	name unknown	150	8
Green, Solomon	pt. Burm's Forrest	48	5
Green, Josias	name unknown	110	5
Green, Moses	pt. Burms Forest	50	8
Gash, Thomas	name unknown	88	9
Grimes, John			4

1783 TAX LIST OF BALTIMORE COUNTY, MARYLAND
Patapsco Lower Hundred

Owner	Tract Name	# Acres	# White Inhabitants
Giles, James	name unknown	59	
Gray, Ephraim	Mashs Rest	147	7
Gray, Comfort	Grays Conveniency	5	4
Gray, Lynch	name unknown	25	4
Govane, James	pt. Hannahs Lot	58	
Gorsuch, David	pt. East Humphreys	131	
	pt. Stones Range	99	12
Griffith, Benjamin	Hailes Folly	12	
	pt. Salisbury Plains	20	
Griffith, Nathan	Wells Angle	200	
	pt. Hails Folly	12	
Gist, Mordecai	pt. Hails Folly	25	
Hail, Meshack			4
Hopkins, Hopkin?			3
Hail, George, Jr.	pt. Gorsuchs Folly	82	
Hanson, Edward	pt. Hansons Wood Lot	130	
Hanson, Jonathan	Mount Royal	300	
	Edwards Lot	50	4
Howard, William			9
Hiser John			8
House, Thomas			4
Hart, John	name unknown	13	
Howard, Ruth	Howells Point	280	
Harrison, Thomas (his heirs)-name unknown		200	
Hopkins, Gerrett of R.	pt. Jobs Addition	150	
Jones, Thomas	name unknown	717	10
Joyce, William			8
Kittleman, Valentine			6
Lynch, Robuck	Plains	226	5
Lux, Darby	name unknown	739	
Laughlin, Robert			4
Lynch, Patrick	name unknown	183	1
Leach, Mary			5
Love, Miles			5
Lane, Richard	pt. Colegates Point	140	
Lynch, William	name unknown	508	
Murphy, Charles			3
Murphy, John			10
Murray, John			10
Maidwell, James	Ensors Inspection	9	
	pt. Merrymans Lot	135	10
Moody, William			4
Rowles, Richard	name is not clear	120	7

1783 TAX LIST OF BALTIMORE COUNTY, MARYLAND
Patapsco Lower Hundred

Owner	Tract Name	# Acres	# White Inhabitants
Maccubbin, William	Maxwells Habitation	240	
	Williams Addition	129	
	Clarrasses Gift	3	
	McCubbins Addition	72	
	Samsons Farm	50	
	Majors Choice	140	
	Morrises Lot	20	5
Marton, Nathan	Kindness Resurveyed	293	8
Merryman, Joseph	Merrymans Lot	105	
	Merrymans Addition	123	8
Merryman, Aberilla	Merrymans Pasture	200	
	Ditto's Discovery	22	
	Todds Delight	48	6
Merryman, John	Morgans Delight	159	
Maidwell, Alexander			5
Moale, John	name unknown	128	
McKinley, Cathe			4
Merryman, Nicholas	Broads Improvement	257	
McFadden, James	Coles Addition	70	
Norwood, Nicholas	name unknown	560	7
Neal, William	name unknown	590	
Neal, Sarah			
Oyston, John	pt. Oystons Choice	15	7
Oyston, Lawrence	pt. Oystons Choice	82	5
Painter, Daniel			3
Perrigoe, Nathan	pt. Burmans Forest	97	8
Perrigoe, John	pt. Burmans Forest	100	6
Peormy?, Henry			4
Pennington, Josias	pt. Addition	70	11
Partridge, John	pt. Good Luck	100	
	Thomas Adventure	83	
	Thomas Range	32	4
Partridge, William	name unknown	230	3
Pearce, John			9
Pearce, Charles			6
Rease, George			2
Rogers, Benjamin	name unknown	248	
Ready, John	pt. Goose Harbor	120	6
Ridgely, Capt. Charles	Sportsmans Hall	570	
	pt. Hails Folly	16	
Rogers, Charles	pt. Morgans Delight	159	
	pt. Gallesbury	30	5
Ryan, Edward			6

1783 TAX LIST OF BALTIMORE COUNTY, MARYLAND
Patapsco Lower Hundred

Owner	Tract Name	# Acres	# White Inhabitants
Rutter, Joseph	pt. Jacobs Lot	23	
	Rutters Folly	15	
	Halls Neglect	25	7
Ridgely, Richard	name unknown	690	
Smith, Patrick			1
Stansbury, Daniel	name unknown	230	7
Sindall, David	Peary's Range	90	4
Spriggs, Richard	name unknown	918	
Sides, Aaron	name unknown	6	7
Stansbury, Richard	Poplar Neck	103	10
Smith, Samuel	name unknown	100	9
Stansbury, Richard Jr.			1
Stansbury, George	name unknown	250	9
Stansbury, Tobias	name unknown	231	4
Shaws, Thomas	pt. Todds Range	50	4
Shaw, Thomas K.	name unknown	81	2
Spear, William	Gorsuches Folly	82	
	Ensors Inspection	30	2
Sollers, Sabrett	name unknown	330	5
Sollers, Joseph	name unknown	225	4
Sollers, Thomas (his heirs)	name unknown	297	10
Sweeting, Edward	Tripple Union	75	7
Sindell, Philip			5
Smith, Job	name unknown	6	6
Smith, Col. Saml.	name unknown	21	
Shields, Abraham			3
Stevenson, John	pt. Edwards & Wills Valleys & Hills	290	8
Stevenson, Mordecai	pt. Edwards & Wills Valleys & Hills	160	4
Stevenson, Sater	pt. Edwards & Wills Valleys & Hills	130	7
Smith, John	pt. East Humphreys	45	5
Smith, Nathaniel	Gays Neglect	15	
Slater, William			11
Taylor, Robert			8
Trotten, Susanna	name unknown	221	3
Turner, Francis			9
Traverse, Col.	Browns Prospect	50	
Todd, Thomas	name unknown	794	9
Todd, Launcelot	pt. Brians Meadows	7	7
Talbott, Benjamin	name unknown	175	5
Toone, John			5

1783 TAX LIST OF BALTIMORE COUNTY, MARYLAND
Patapsco Lower Hundred

Owner	Tract Name	# Acres	# White Inhabitants
Vanbibber, Abraham	Paradise	28	
	name unknown	92	
Wilkinson, William	name unknown	487	8
Wells, Joseph	pt. Pearrys Range	10	6
Woodard, James	Harrymans Pasture	42	6
Watts, John	name unknown	50	5
Watts, Sarah	name unknown	20	2
Woolrick, Philip	Fox Hall	100	6
Weeb, Brown			5
Wheeler, John	pt. Morgans Delight	50	4
Woodward, Thomas	name unknown	199	3

Paupers in Patapsco Lower Hundred

Norwood, Mary-3
Burm, William -3
Sterrett, Charles -4
Fin, Peter -2
Taylor, Philip -3
Page, John -5
Case, Frederick -2
Simcock, Theophilus -2
Harryman, Caleb -4
Nosil, Margaret -3
Glen, Samuel -2
Rowles, Ruth -6
Hirast ?, John -3
Rainbow, Charles -3
Ritaker, Adam -3

Caum, Aaron-2
Watkins, Samuel-7
Burn, Michael-4
Cathart, Samuel -3
West, Charity -2
Brumpft, Benjamin -5
Alterfrit, Jacob -4
Benjamin, John -3
Hardley, John -1
Perine, William -2
Rogers, James -7
Griffith, Margaret -3
Johnson, Thomas -4
Walker, David -7
With, William -4

Ferrow, Stephen-2
Dizard, John-6
Holmes, John -2
Howard, John -7
Leggitt, Henry -2
Hadley, John -6
Cole, John -3
Steel, John -2
Simpson, Samuel -2
Sergent, John -5
Rain, John -5
Person, John -1
Perkins, Mary -3
Green, Ruth -3
Doyle, Thomas -5

1783 TAX LIST OF BALTIMORE COUNTY, MARYLAND
Pipe Creek Hundred

Owner	Tract Name	# Acres	# White Males	# White Inhabitants
Ashman, Ann				
Ambrose, William	Sapling Ridge?	205	1	3
Ambrose, William Jr.	Saplin Ridge	160	1	5
Algier, John	pt. Ribbles Folly	179	1	8
Aler? Jacob	pt. Wells Care	149	1	5
Adams, William			1	3
Ailer, Ulrick	North Canton	310		
	New Switzerland	57		
	Water Oak Level	47	1	5
Algier, Jacob	Jacobs Beginning	86	1	10
Bond, Benjamin			1	4
Belt, Joseph	Fair Play	142	1	6
Belt, John Jr.			1	6
Belt, Leonard	pt. Addition to Elleges Farm	72		
	Certificate	192	1	9
Burns, James			1	4
Bentley, Zachariah			1	2
Butler, Nicholas	pt. Butlers Farm	150	1	6
Butler, 'mon Jr.	pt. Butlers Farm	150	1	8
Beck, Daniel	pt. I Will and Will Not	26	1	5
Baxter, Charity	Baxters Choice	190	1	9
Bonney, Josiah			1	6
Brittain, Nicholas	Not named	100		
Baxter, Samuel	pt. Baxters Choice	110	1	7
Brown, John	Browns Recovery	22		
	Beaver Hall	9		
	Pleasant Grove	50	1	5
Brown, Richard	pt. Wee Bitt	104	1	1
Brown, Edward	pt. German Town	80		
Brown, George	pt. Wee Bit	180		
	Foxes Thickett	29	1	5
Blizzard, William	Blizzards Bottom	52		
	Lanes 'ddition	50		
	White Oak Bottom	20	?	4
Blizzard, John			1	8
Brown, Hugh			1	6
Bomgardner, John	not named	14	1	3
Bell, William	pt. New Germany	300		
Brown, Henry	Bockland Enlarged	423	1	3
Brown, John Jr.	Johns Lot	82	1	7
Brown, William	Snake Den	84	1	9
Boy, Jeremiah			1	11

-88-

1783 TAX LIST OF BALTIMORE COUNTY, MARYLAND
Pipe Creek Hundred

Owner	Tract Name	# Acres	# White Males	# White Inhabitants
Brown, William of Geo.			1	4
Brown, George	not named	150		
Bower, Christian	North Canton	65		
	Little Proffit	25		
Beckley, Henry			1	7
Belt, Jeremiah			1	5
Burns, John	Pleasant Garden	48		
	Winchesters Lot	186		
	Burns Lot	30		
	Done In Time	30		
	Meadows Green	14		
	Burns Meadow	6		
	Shitleys Lane	121	1	5
Bailey, John (guardian of William Bailey of Enoch)	pt. Butlers Farm	120	1	11
Baker, John			1	3
Bond, John of Chestnut Ridge-land not named		93		
Bush, Shadrack	Mothers Friendship	40		
Bush, Sarah			1	2
Blaze, Isaac			1	5
Bruce, Norman	pt. Iron Intention	1000		
Butler, Amon Sr.	pt. Hailes Adventure	564		
Connely, James	pt. Greens Goodwill	225	1	14
Creter, Martin			1	5
Creagh, John	pt. Addition to Elledges Farm	212		
Casey, John-Bachelor	Sec. was David Holton			
Crouder, Ely			1	4
Corbin, Benjamin	not named	100	1	10
Corbin, Elijah-Bachelor	Sec. was Joshua Kelley			
Conneley, Jonathan-Bachelor, Sec. was Francis Matthews				
Crammitt, Martin	pt. Cromwells Desire	92	1	4
Cooper, Vincent	McGills Choice	126	1	6
Catore, Peter			1	4
Davis, Joshua-Bachelor	Sec. was Abraham Lane			
Dorson, William			1	2
Dean, Jacob			1	8
Decker, Frederick	pt. Winchesters Lot	228	1	3
Day, Mark	Manheim Town	50	1	7
Day, Isaac	Hookers Meadows Resurveyed	213	1	7
Day, John			1	4
Dean, John	Frugality	95	1	3
Doyle, Richard	Morrows Venture	158	1	10
Ensor, John			1	4

1783 TAX LIST OF BALTIMORE COUNTY, MARYLAND
Pipe Creek Hundred

Owner	Tract Name	# Acres	# White Males	# White Inhabitants
Deale, Philip	Woodhome	50		
	Philipsburgh	25		
	Rock Meadow	25		
	Wrights Range	50		
	pt. Bite the Biter	120	1	10
Duckhart, Volerious	pt. Greens Goodwill	225		
Everhart, George	pt. Wells Care Enlarged	100		
	Klinks Stoney Meadows	32		
	Klinks Addition	38		
	Halls Addition	15		
	Everharts Addition	16	1	7
Epaugh, Henry			1	5
Ensor, Abraham	not named	150		
Franks, Philip	pt. I Will & I Will Not	76 1/2		
	Gramores Addition	23		
	Shenough	10		
	Bottle Hill	25	1	10
Fouble, Melchor			1	6
Fouble, Michael			1	6
Frog, Boston	Frogs Forrest	103	1	12
Fetterly, Jacob			1	4
Frankford, Nicholas	not named	311	1	10
Fisher, John	Johns Pleasure	70	1	5
Forney, Mark	pt. Wells Care Enlarged	168		
Forney, Philip	pt. Wells Care Enlarged	158		
Fisher, John Jr.			1	4
Fisher, George	Tipperara	160		
	Friendship	147	1	11
Fisher, Leonard-Bachelor, Sec. was George Fisher				
Fisher, Michael	Clareys New Holland	329		
	pt. Cornells Desire with Mine Bank-10		1	3
Foreman, Leonard	not named	102	1	2
Fryfogle, Stophel			1	11
Franch, George	Castle Hannah & Geo. Fancy	516		
Finley, Thomas	pt. Elledges Farm	140		
Frazier, John	Charles Delight	50	1	2
Fauble, Frederick-Bachelor, Sec. was Peter Fauble				
Gore, Andrew			1	4
Gore, John			1	2
Gore, Michael	pt. Nicholsons Manor	127		
Gore, Christian			1	7
Gill, Edward of Stephen	pt. Thomas Choice	100	1	3

1783 TAX LIST OF BALTIMORE COUNTY, MARYLAND
Pipe Creek Hundred

Owner	Tract Name	# Acres	# White Males	# White Inhabitants
Gill, Thomas	pt. Thomas Choice	100	1	4
Gill, Stephen	pt. Thomas Choice	100	1	3
Gill, John Jr.	pt. Butlers Farm	124	1	3
Green, Henry-bachelor	Sec. was Jonathan Plowman			
Greenland, Moses	pt. Hurtleberry Ridge	100	1	4
Gunkell, Michael	pt. Irones Intention	80		
	pt. Hickory Resurveyed	45		
Grammer, John			1	4
Gorsuch, Loveless	pt. Rochester	150	1	1
Gorsuch, Thomas	pt. Buck Range	150		
Gross, Francis	Betty France	135	1	3
Gist, Col. Thomas	not named	459 1/2		
Gist, Joshua	not named	100		
Gill, John	Nancys Fancy	24		
	Buck Harbour	347		
	Narrow Ridge	35		
Hannakay, Jesse			1	3
Holton, David			1	9
Howard, William-bachelor, Security was Ely Crowder				
Harris, William	pt. Hookers Meadows &			
	pt. I Will & I Will Not	243	1	3
Hions, William	McQueens Choice	35	1	3
Hess, Peter	pt. Hickory Ridge	60	1	4
Hayes, Jos'h.	pt. Rochester	90		
	Gills Prospect	40		
	Pleasant Meadows	20		
	Lovealis Add. & Mills	10	1	7
Holmes, Jas.?	pt. Rochester	225	1	9
Holmes Jas./Jon'a?	pt. Rochester	150	1	7
Haghn, Michael	Harrs? Meadow	18		
	Harrs? Choice	60		
	High Spring	50		
	Dutch Land	50		
	pt. Frankford	252	1	9
Haghn, Adam			1	3
Houck, Michael	Potters Lot	150	1	5
Haun, Paul	pt. Intended Friendship	38	1	7
Houk, Esther	pt. Wells Care	136	1	5
Hammond, William			1	5
Heney, Stophel	Stoffields Delight	108		
	Jerry Pear?	318	1	5
Heney Stoffield Jr.			1	4
Harris, George			1	7

1783 TAX LIST OF BALTIMORE COUNTY, MARYLAND
Pipe Creek Hundred

Owner	Tract Name	# Acres	# White Males	# White Inhabitants
Hooker, Thomas	Come By Chance	4 1/2		
	Hookers Meadows	67 1/2		
	Point Look Out	100		
	Hookers Enlargement	240		
	Vaughans Level	20		
	Hookers Hope	33 1/2		
	Shraders Desire	8		
	Hookers Liberty	10 1/2	1	9
Hudson, Jonathan	not named	500		
Helms, Mayberry	not named	300		
Holliday, John Robert	not named	600		
Hicks, Stephen	pt. Hickory Ridge	33		
James, Thomas	pt. Rochester	100	1	8
James, William	Stains Neglect	103	1	8
Jones, John	not Named	170		
Joy, Peter	not named	90	1	6
Kelley, Joshua	Wests Lot	50		
	Mount Pleasant	25		
	pt. Jones Discovery	90	1	7
Kelley, James	pt. Jones Discovery	60		
	Pleasant Valley	50		
	pt. Plowmans Park	55	1	11
Keefer, John	Good Neighborhood	30		
King, William	Piney Meadows	83 1/2		
Louderslager, Philip	Hidelburgh	50		
	Louderslagers Meadows	25		
	pt. Petticoats Loose	74	1	7
Louderslager, George	not named	50	1	2
Louderslager, Martin			1	3
Loveall, Henry	not named	93	1	11
Lane, Samuel	Deans Comfort	54		
	pt. Hickory Ridge Resurveyed	69		
	pt. Rochester	40	1	11
Loveall, Ethan	pt. Hickory Ridge	125	1	5
Loveall, Zebulon	Chestnut Level	104	1	4
Loveall, Luther	Luthers Delight	137	1	9
Loveall, William	pt. Hickory Ridge	100	1	6
Lane, Abraham	pt. Rochester	30	1	4
Lane, John	pt. Rochester	17		
	Millers Gain	9 1/2	1	3
Lippo, Jacob	pt. Ribbles Meadow	80	1	4
Littear, Jacob	Pottsburgh	158	1	11
Lippo, George	Fredericksburg	55	1	3

1783 TAX LIST OF BALTIMORE COUNTY, MARYLAND
Pipe Creek Hundred

Owner	Tract Name	# Acres	# White Males	# White Inhabitants
Lux, Capt. Darby	Sportsmans Hall	825		
Lyon, William	not named	400		
Murray, John	pt. Elledges Farm	398		
	pt. Nicholsons Manor	52		
	Carrs Chance	64		
	Carrs Discovery	27 1/4	1	8
Murray, Christopher	Murrays Favor	100		
	Add. to Joshuas Lott	97		
	pt. Add. to Elledges Farm	146		
	Land of Promise	53	1	4
Murray, James	Hookers Chance	50		
	pt. Add. to Elledges Farm	104	1	7
Murray, Shadrack	pt. Add. to Elledges Farm	202		
	pt. Butlers Farm	235	1	6
Marsh, Richard			1	4
Matthews, Francis			1	3
Murray, William			1	1
Munch, Adam	Cudlow	75	1	4
Myers, Isaac	pt. Wee Bit	125	1	9
Miller, Henry	pt. Wee Bit	125	1	9
Merryman, Benjamin	not named	200		
Myers, George	not named	479		
Matthews, Thomas	pt. Add. to Elledges Farm with Grist & mercht mills	200	1	6
Moore, James			1	3
Nash, John			1	10
Netherclift, William			1	3
Nace, Peter			1	6
Osborne, Joseph	Turkey Cock Hall	34		
	Ellidges Folly	50		
	pt. Elledges Farm	106	1	8
Osborne, John	pt. Osbornes Lot	48		
	pt. Sportsmans Hall	73	1	10
Osborne, Daniel	pt. Daniels Delight	50		
	Richards Chance	45		
	Daniels Choice	43 1/2		
	pt. Butlers Farm	74	1	9
Orr, John			1	5
Oats, Henry	Hogshead	150 1/2		
	Henry Oats Lot	27	1	12
Oats, Peter	pt. Winchesters Lot	239	1	11
Owings, Samuel	Prt of Everything Needful	1300		

1783 TAX LIST OF BALTIMORE COUNTY, MARYLAND
Pipe Creek Hundred

Owner	Tract Name	# Acres	# White Males	# White Inhabitants
Pierly, Conrad	New Town	200	1	6
Pierly, Ludowick	Ludwicks Berry	72	1	2
Plowman, Jonathan	Plowmans Park	339	1	5
Peachy, James			1	2
Plowman, James	Jonathans Meadow	150	1	7
Plowman, Edward	pt. Plowmans Park	196	1	3
Price, John			1	7
Pixley, Jacob	land and mill	172	1	12
Ports, Philip	pt. Mountain Town	200	1	9
Plowman, John	Plowmans Fancy	180	1	2
Pierly, Peter			1	3
Plowman, Jonathan Jr.	not named	196		
Petticoat, Nicholas			1	3
Reese, Adam	Small's Delight	75		
	Reeses Trial	50		
	pt. Wee Bitt	62	1	8
Robinson, John	Rotterdam	16	1	3
Ribble, John	Planton	65	1	2
Roof, Michael	Petty Spring	31	1	7
Richart, John	pt. Stoney Meadows	200	1	5
Ritter, Ludowick			1	1
Ritter, John	Nova Scotia	224	1	2
Ritter, Michael	pt. Abrahams Garden	150	1	3
Roop, Jacob	Tetrix? Folly	115	1	3
Rinehart, Tetrick			1	3
Richards, Richard Jr.			1	3
Richards, Samuel			1	2
Richards, Capt. Richard	Illinois	128		
	Jacobs Pasture	14		
	Transylvania	195		
	Batchelors Choice	50		
	Richards Rectitude	37		
	Rattlesnake Hill	50		
	Corn Hill Reserved	525		
	The Shades	5 1/2		
	The Parade	32		
	New Market	67		
	Pinsent? Will	30		
	Fertile Meadows	147		
	Richards Conclusion	50		
	Fingalls Enosier?	93		
	Modicum	12 1/2	1	9
Rhodes, Matthias			1	1

1783 TAX LIST OF BALTIMORE COUNTY, MARYLAND
Pipe Creek Hundred

Owner	Tract Name	# Acres	# White Males	# White Inhabitants
Richards, Nicholas-bachelor, Security was Capt. Richard Richards				
Snap, Peter	Overprone	120	1	5
Stiger, Andrew	Rope Walk	414		
Snider, Martin	Petticoats Lodge	146	1	2
Snider, Michael			1	5
Snider, Frederick	pt. Petticoats Lodge	116	1	4
Snider, Abraham			1	5
Sellars, Sabritt	Lasting Pasture	100		
	pt. Elledges Farm	66		
	Add. to William	100		
	pt. Goodwill	32		
	pt. William Refused	161		
	Hookers Fancy	22 1/2		
	pt. Butlers Farm	113		
Snider, Christopher	pt. I Will & I Will Not	128	1	4
Sherner? John	pt. German Town	150	1	6
Storm, Jacob			1	4
Smith, Michael			1	4
Sapp, Daniel			1	7
Strickland, Thomas			1	5
Sich?, Benjamin	not named	75	1	4
Sich?, Joseph	not named	61	1	3
Staines, Thomas	pt. Rochester	12		
Stansbury, Jacob	Hogg Harbour	123	1	3
Salbowker?, Henry	Upper Hagreton	55 1/4		
	pt. Stoney Valley	140		
	Morning Choice	5		
	Land Raw	31	1	8
Sterrip, Peter	pt. Stoney Valley	70	1	6
Sollers, Paul	pt. Everything Needful	100	1	12
Sense, Christian	Meeleys Delight	68		
	Christians Delight	10		
	pt. Winsaw	50	1	9
Sense, Christian Jr.-bachelor, Security was Christian Sense				
Sense, Adam			1	3
Shaver, John	Johns Hope	200	1	7
Shaver, Jacob			1	2
Shrier, Kinyes	pt. Wifes Mill	141	1	7
Spittler, John			1	7
SHowers, Henry-bachelor, Security was John Showers				
Shuster, Catherine	Franshofen	109	1	3
Shuster, Josh'a			1	5
Slagle, Margaret			1	7

-95-

1783 TAX LIST OF BALTIMORE COUNTY, MARYLAND
Pipe Creek Hundred

Owner	Tract Name	# Acres	# White Males	# White Inhabitants
Showers, John	pt. Winchesters Lot	237		
	Transylvania	265		
	Stephens Hope	250		
	High Barney	50		
	Bladenshome	25		
	Rustehoof?	48 1/2		
	Berlein?	25		
	Cradeys? Neighbors	39		
	pt. Pleasant Garden	15		
	Seaport	14	1	8
Storey, Thomas	Friendship	75	1	8
Scales, John	Spring Garden	102	1	6
Stevens, Abraham	Deans Delight	80		
	New Found Bottom	189	1	7
Sharpe, Horatio	pt. Holes Adventure	1700		
Stansbury, John	not named	77		
Stevenson, Richard	not named	100		
Thomas, Charles			1	2
Thorpe, Thomas			1	6
Troyer, George	pt. German Town	72	1	5
Troyer, George Jr.-bachelor, Security was George Troyer				
Troyer, Jacob	pt. German Town	91	1	1
Tomer, Christopher(Christian?)-pt. Iron Intention		220	1	7
Tomer, John			1	2
Turner, John			1	12
Tanner, George			1	6
Uppercoe, Jacob	Smiths Spring	180		
	Impark	65		
	pt. I Will & I Will Not	18	1	3
Underwood, Nehemiah			1	5
Vaugh, Richard			1	5
Wooden, Stephen	pt. Daniels Delight	100		
	Gists Inheritance	15 1/2		
	pt. Daniels Choice	25	1	8
Westley, John,-bachelor, Security was Henry Westley				
Westley, Henry			1	3
Welch, Leah			1	9
Walker, Thomas	not named	378	1	7
Wiggott, Andrew	pt. Rochester	12		
Woolf, Leonard			1	7
Weaver, George	Pallentine	45		
	Stoney Hills	10		
	Shroads Range	18	1	6

1783 TAX LIST OF BALTIMORE COUNTY, MARYLAND
Pipe Creek Hundred

Owner	Tract Name	# Acres	# White Males	# White Inhabitants
Weaver, John	pt. Tipperary	200	1	7
Weaver, Philip	pt. United Friendship	11-1/2		
	pt. Cromwells Desire	65	1	7
Wybland, Charles			1	5
Wilmot, John	pt. Rochester	1000		
Wilmot, Robert	not named	1000		
Worthing, Samuel	not named	170		
Winchester, William	not named	37		
Young, James of B'r Town	Hales Adventure	586		
Yinglins, John	pt. Johns Pleasure	10	1	7

PAUPERS

Berry, John 1-2
Musgrove, Edward 1-5

Roberts, John 1-2
Swords, Hugh 1-2
West, Thomas 1-6

Shriver, David
Thompson, Ab'm 1-7

INDEX TO THE TRACT NAMES

Abners Delight 18
Abrahams Choice 73
Abrahams Exception 68
Abrahams Garden 94
Abrahams Pleasure 26, 31
Abrahams Ridge 74
Abrams Pleasure 35
Abirillers Fancy 40
Abrelers Garden 36
Absoloms Meadows 47
Affinty & Abriteres Garden 30
Adam 81
Adams Garden 15
Addition 52, 55, 67, 85
Africa 2
Alborough 37
Albrow 42
Aletheas Lot 52
Alexanders Range 2
Allmoneys Meadows 64
Aman Inheritance 17
Ammons Forrest 80
Andersons Lot 64
Andersons Intention 64
Andersons Retreat 69
Andrews Care 37
Andrews Neglect 37
Angels Fortune 46
Annapolis 32, 35
Ansells Lot 64
Anthonys Delight 51
Anthonys Hope 79
Arabia Felix 19
Arabia Petre Enlarged 19
Archibalds Level 81
Archibalds Meadow 74
Arions Folly 72
Arions Prospect 72
Arnolds Desire 18
Arnolds Harbour 13
Art of Everything Needful 93
Arthurs Choice 37, 41
Arthurs Lot 26
Ashers Purchase 37, 38
Auchentoroly 44

Authors Choice 39
B. Manor 30, 32, 33
Batchelors Choice 94
Bachelors Delight 1
Bachelor Hall 36
Bachelors Choice 60
Bachelors Neck 61
Bachelors Prospect 61
Bachelors Ridge 39
Bacon Hall 56, 72, 79
Bakers Discovery 14, 15, 17
Balistone 5, 6, 7
Balistones Support 6
Banks Delight 50
Barbadoes 17
Bare Hills 44, 58
Barneys Ridge 82
Barren Hills 77
Barnes Level 14
Barretts Addition 59
Barretts Delight 59
Bertons Mount 38
Baseman's-Beasman's
　Discovery 13, 14, 17
Bashan 18
Batchelors Meadows 37
Bathany Cambria 27
Batsons Forest 53
Battle Ray 55
Baxters Choice 88
Baxtons Forest 61
Bazils Prospect 81
Bear Neck 38
Beasman (see Baseman)
Beaver Hall 88
Beavers 1st Bottom 73
Beavers 2nd Bottom 73
Beavers Range 79
Beavers Retirement 73
Bedetton 55
Belfast 75
Bells 66
Bells Discovery 55
Bells Lot 64, 65
Benjamins Beginning 53

Benjamins Choice 78
Benjamins Discovery 14
Benj. Hills & Valleys 58
Benjamins Lot 66
Benjamins Mill Lot 44
Bennets Grievance 18
Bennetts Park 13
Berlein 96
Bessons Plott 72
Bethel 69
Betty France 91
Bettys Adventure 49
Biddersons Neck 1
Big Spring 76
Bills Meadows 68
Binnexs Chance 49
Birelers Fancy, 38
Bitchdons Delight 5
Bite The Biter 17, 53, 90
Bivens Adventure 37
Bivens Discovery 40
Black Woolf Neck 38, 42
Bladens 31, 32
Bladenshome 96
Bladens M. 31
Bladens Manor 34, 68
Bladesn M. 31
Blathana Cambury 54
Blathany Cambry 51
Blizzards Bottom 88
Blue Mount 74
Blunder 45
Bockland Enlarged 88
Bollers Adventure 33
Bonds Care 37
Bonds Folly 68
Bonds Forrest 19, 20, 26, 32
Bonds Garrison 44, 47, 48
Bonds Hazard 72
Bonds Industry 49, 60
Bonds Inheritance 49
Bonds Lot Enlarged 6
Bonds Neck 37, 38, 40, 42
Bonds Pleasant Hills 47
Bonds Water Mills 31, 36

Bonnets Park 19
Boot 77
Borings Landing 1
Borings Meadows 78
Borings Range 72,76,81,82
Borings Struggle 73
Bosleys Chance 74
Bosleys Expectation 42
Bosleys Lot 64
Bosleys Plains 64
Bosleys Policy 54
Bottle Hill 90
Bought Dearer 53
Brattens Begining 81
Brians Meadows 86
Bring Me Home 57
Britain Ridge 51
Britains Meadows 51
Broad Meadow 60
Broads Chance 50
Broads Design 52
Broads Improvement 6,85
Broads Meadows 52
Brooks Adventure 13
Brooks Cross 26,27,30,31,35
Brooks Kindness 61
Brothers Choice 41,45
Browns Farm 34
Browns Prospect 86
Browns Recovery 88
Browns Sharp 18
Brunts 67
Bryans Chance 82
Bryans Meadows 82
Buchanans Palace 50
Buck Range 91
Buck Ridge 80
Bucking 13
Bucks Forrest 14,17
Bucks Goodwill 17
Bucks Outlet 64
Bucks Park 13,14,15,18
Bucks Purchase 53
Bucks Range 3,14,18,64, 74,75
Bud 57

Buffoloe 52
Burmans Forest 85
Burns Forrest 83
Burns Lot 89
Burns Meadow 89
Burtons Land 30
Busbys Chance 72
Busbys Plott 72
Bushy Neck 2
Bussey Jesse 27
Butlers Farm 88,89,91,93,95
Buttons Adventure 19
Caladonia 14,15,16,18
Calaforna 72,78,82 & Calafornia
Cambridge 32,33
Cambells Search 13
Canaan 18,53
Candle 80
Caples Dilligence 73
Caples Pleasant Bottom 73
Carrick Fergus 14,16
Carrolls 66,67,68
Carrolls Manor 64,65,66,67, 68,69
Carrols Upland 38
Carrolls Adventure 31
Carrolls Scrutiney 37
Carrs Chance 93
Carrs Discovery 93
Carrs Lot 59
Carters Rock 29
Case Is Altered 42
Casebolts Delight 61
Casestones Choice 39
Castle Calder 74
Castle Hannah 90
Caswells Venture 39
Catherines Chance 76
Causil Resurveyed 82
Certificate 56,61,72,76, 80,88
Chamberlains Meadows 66
___ Chance 73
Chance 3,50,55,72
Chaneys Ramble 72

Charles Chance 68
Charles Delight 90
Charles Luck 15
Charles Policy 49
Chatsworth 46,47
Cherry Garden 2
Chestnut Level 92
Chestnut Neck 41
Chevy or Chavey Chase 3, 5,50,55
Christeen Creek 77
Christians Delight 95
Christophers Lott 51
Christofers Habitation 74
Cimney Hill 41
Clareys New Holland 90
Clarks Forest 27
Clarksons Hope 26,30,35
Clarrasses Gift 85
Coales Discover 2
Cockermouth 19
Cockeys Delight 50
Cockeys Folly 58
Cockeys Lot 50
Cockeys Recovery 50
Cockeys Trust 50
Cold Friday 57
Cold Saturday 16
Cole Chapter 76
Cole Pitt 76
Colegate Dye Owings & Charlotta Dye Colegates Add. 57
Colegates Last Shift 83
Colegates Point 83,84
Coles Addition 85
Coles Adventure 44,45,46,47
Coles Bottom 81
Coles Caves & Mill 50
Coles Chance 53
Coles Discovery 51
Coles Frolic 74
Coles Good Luck Resurveyed 51
Coles Manor 34
Coles Meadows 75,79

-99-

Coles Mountain 74
Coles Prospect 78
Coles Search Amended 53
Coles Struggle 51
Colle Stones Chance 41
Colletts Adventure 69
Come By Chance 2, 31, 45, 92
Conclusion 57
Condem'd For A Mile 33
Connaways Venture 14
Connellys Delight 56
Conners Delight 16
Constable 38
Constitution Hills 44
Continuance 7
Contrivance 53, 76
Cooks Adventure 46
Cooks Desire 14
Cooks End 67
Cooksons Content 46
Cooksons Polygon 48
Corbins Rest 83
Corn Hill Reserved 94
Cornells Desire 90
Costly 19
Cotts Mine 16
Cows Hill 51
Coxes Farm 74
Coxes Park 80
Coxs Pleasant Meadows 74
Coxes Privilege 2
Coxs Fancy 29
Coxs Hope 36
Coxs Prospect 54
Cradeys Neighbors 96
Cromwells Addition 56
Cromwells Chance 46, 47, 56
Cromwells Desire 89, 97
Cromwells Neck 57
Cromwells Park 60
Cross' Chance 15
Crosses Choice 61
Crosses Grove 78
Crosses Park 77
Cub Hill 38
Cuckoldmakers Hill 37
* College 50
* out of order

Cudlow 93
Cumberland 17, 50, 51, 54
Dales & Valleys 60
Danby 5
Danby Hills 38
Daniels Choice 93, 96
Daniels Delight 93, 96
Daniels Plains 1
Daniels Town & Watters 37, 39
Daniels Whimsey 46
Darbyshire 44, 46
Darley Hall 7, 83
Darnells Camp 38, 42
Darnells Sylvania 42
Davi 67
David's Hope 17
Davis Chance 75
Davis Farm 14
Days Choice 75
Days Lott 68, 69
Dead Mans Advent 55
Deans Comfort 92
Deans Delight 96
Dear Bit 1, 5, 6
Deep Valley 20
Deer Park 16, 47
Deer Park & Trouting Streams 19
Delaney 27, 30
Delaneys 31, 32, 34
Demitts Choice 31
Demmitts Delight 29
Denmark 15
Discovery 54, 81
Discovery Mountain 54
Dispute Ended 18
Ditto's Addition 64
Ditto's Discovery 85
Ditto's Hope 37
Dixons 4, 6
Dixons Chance 42
Dixons Relief 6
Done In Time 89
Donmark 17
Dorseys Plains 75
Double Trouble 5
Dowleys Range 15

Downes Lott 66
Drumk Hasle 54
Drunkards Hall 58
Duck Harbor 3
Dublin 31
Dukes Palace 39
Dukes Discovery 2
Dulaney 29, 36
Dulaneys 28, 30, 36
Dunkers Lott 16
Durkins Adventure 37
Dusty Miller & B'Ds.
  Addition 57
Dutch 38
Dutch Land 91
Dyes Delight 51
East Humphreys 84, 86
Ebenezers Park 37
Edenburough 15
Edward's & Wills Valleys
  & Hills 86
Edwards Chance 75
Edwards Lott 84
Edwards Venture 18
Egypt 1, 6
Egypt Enlarged 59
Eleanors Lookout 57
Elijahs Lott 82
Elizabeths Delight 66
Elizabeths Diligence 45
Elizabeths Purchase 36
Elizes Grove 57
Elks Range 38
Elledges Farm (Elleges)
  77, 88, 89, 90, 93, 95
Ellens Lot 67
Ellidges Folly
Elliott Risk, 29
Elliotts Chance, 69
Enlargement 47, 67
Enloes Choice 38
Enloes Desire 31
Enloes Shift 31
Ensigns Grove 45
Ensors Inspection 83,
  84, 86

-100-

Ensors Study 5	Friendship Completed 16	Gossicks Choice 59
Escape 13,17	Frizzles Choice 69	Gotts Grove 72
Esenburgh 76	Frogs Forrest 90	Gotts Hope 54
Eve 77	Frugality 89	Gramores Addition 90
Everharts Addition 90	Fruitful Meadows 64	Graves End 67
Everitts Friendship 14	Fugates Folly 64	Grays Covenience 84
Everitts Progress 18	Fullers Outlet 37	Green Land 53
Everything Needful 95	Gads Delight 29	Green Spring Forest 50
Executors Management 68	Gallaways Hope 39	Green Spring Punch 57
Eye Sore 37	Gallaways Inlargement 39	Green Springs 66
F. Delight & Ruth Garden 30	Gallesbury 85	Greens Desire 72,73,79
Fair Dealing 61	Galley Pot Level 45	Greens Discovery 36
Fair Play 75,88	Game Plenty 16	Greens Goodwill 89,90
Farvers Favour 4	Gassaways 27	Greens Fancy 80
Fathers Gift 19	Gassaways Ridge 36	Greens Improvement 33
Faubles Barren Hills 76	Gays Inspection 5,38,40,41,	Greens Neglect 33
Faubles Garden 76	53,59	Greens Park 33
Fellowship 54,59	Gays Neglect 86	Greens Palace 66
Fellowship Resurveyed 58	Gays Timber Wood 26	Greens Patent 66
Fellsdale 19	Georges 16	Greens Safeguard 54
Fertile Meadows 94	Geo. Fancy 90	Grimm Garden 68
Fiddle Stick 39	Georges 80	Groses Outlet 41
Fields Forest 1	Georges Improvement 61	Groves 55
Find Me Out 56	Georges Lott 15	Grovers Meadows 64
Fingalls Enosier 94	German Town 88,95,96	Guindle Woul 75
Flag Meadow 15,16,18	Germany 46	Gunners Range 54,60
Fords Choice 53,55,76	Giest Silvania 15	Gunpowder Manor 28,30,32
Fords Folly 73	Gift 3	33,36
Fords Friendship 53	Gills Prospect 91	Gutherys Chance 31
Forecast 49	Gists Inheritance 96	Hab Nab At A Venture 2
Forked Meadows 66	Gists Search 49,53,55,58	Hab Nab Enlarged 57
Forrest 54,60	Gittings Choice 30	Hails (Hales) Folly 83,85
Forrest Level 14,15	Golden Mine 38	Hales (Hailes) Adventure 54
Fortune 3	Good Hope 42	77,89,96,97
Fosters Hunting Ground 81	Good Life 38	Hales Park 56
Foubles Lott 76	Good Luck 52,54,58,72,	Halls Addition 90
Fox Hall 28,83,87	77,85	Halls 1st Design 54
Foxes Thickett 88	Good Neighbourhood 14,19,	Halls Neglect 86
Francis Choice 40	(Neighborhood) 92	Hammonds Meadows 13
Frankford 91	Goodwill 95	Hannahs Lot 82,84
Franklins Purchase 2,7	Goose Harbor 85	Hansons Wood Lot 84
Franshofen 95	Gorsuches Adventure 53	Hap Hazard 7,46
Fraziers Delight 72	Gorsuchs-(Gorsuches)	Happy Be Lucky 46
Fredericksburg 92	Folly 84,86	Harbour 1
Friends Discovery 55	Goshen 3,55	Hard Lion 42
Friendship 50,53,58,90,96	Gosicks Folly 7	Hares Meadows 50

* Fat Brussells 56
* out of order

Harriford 57	Hog Pen Hills 50	Inloes Lone 2
Harrimans Desire 1	Hog Island 75,79	Inloes Rest 38,40
Harrimans Outlet 2	Hog Range 13	Intended Friendship 91
Harrimons Best Way 54	Hogg Harbour 95	Ipstone 75,79
Harrimons Frolic 39	Hogshead 93	Iron Intention 89,96
Harrisons Meadows 49,61	Holeys Neck 3	Irones Intention 91
Harrs Choice 91	Honesty's Best Policy 26	Isaacs Retirement 15
Harrs Meadow 91	Honesty's Neighbors 30	Island 42
Harrymans Pasture 87	Hookers Adventure 57	Ivory Hill 54
Hawkins Desire 45	Hookers Adventure 57	Ivy Hills 44
Hawkins Fancy 15	Hookers Chance 93	Jacksons Chance 44
Hays Choice 66	Hookers Enlargement 92	Jacobs Beginning 88
Hazard 3,4	Hookers Fancy 95	Jacobs Desighn 80
Head & Tail 81	Hookers Farm 57	Jacobs Fancy 77
Heathcotes Cottage 34	Hookers Hope 92	Jacobs Garden 80
Heidleburgh 75,77	Hookers Lasting Pasture 51	Jacobs Inheritance 42
Helmore 50,58,59	Hookers Liberty 92	Jacobs Lott 26,86
Helmores Addition 50	Hookers Meadows 16,19,89,	Jacobs Pasture 94
Hemps Mile 73	91,92	Jamaica 26,31,36
Hendons Hope 31	Hookers Prospect 72	Jamaica Mans Plague 46
Henry Oats Lot 93	Hookers Prosperity 61	James & Robsons Delight 52
Henrys Chance 79	Hope 45	James Beginning 41
Henrys Delight In A___s 50	Hopesons Choice 83	James Chance 27
Henrys Folly 73,76	Hopewell 2,7	James Delight 29
Henrys Meadows 80	Hopyard 47,48,53	James Fore Cast 42
Herriford 17	Horn Point 42	James Forest 32
Hickory Bottom 53	Hotes Outlet Amended 74	James Lot 28,75
Hickory Resurveyed 91	Howells Point 84	James Park 31,37,39,41
Hickory Ridge 91,92	Hughes Addition 66	James Prospect 52,56
Hicks Addition 26	Hughes Lot 66	Jenkins Purchase 32
Hicks Adventure 26	Hughes Prospect 66	Jeopardy 60,61
Hicks Folly 55	Hunting Ground 38	Jerrah 52
Hicks Forest 55	Hunting Quarter 41	Jerry Pear 91
Hidelburgh 92	Hunts Adventure 66	Jobs Addition 84
High Barney 96	Hursts Hills 77	John & Thomas' Forest 51,
High Germany 3	Hurtleberry Ridge 91	57,58
High Spring 91	Hutchins Addition 65,68	Johns Adventure 78
Hills & Dales 72	Hutchins Lott 27,66	Johns Chance 14,18
Hills & Hollows 68	Hutchins Neglect 27	Johns Dale 50
Hills & Valleys 61	Hutsons Forrest 15	John's Habitation 37
Hills Camp 27,35	I Know Not 61	Johns Hope 95
Hills Forest 27,35	I Will & I Will Not 88,90,91,	Johns Lot 88
Hilly Run 74	95,96	Johns Pleasure 90,97
Hinds Desire 39	Illinois 94	Johnsburgh 81
Hines Purchase 3	Impark 96	Join All 79
Hobsons Choice 74,83	Inclosure 53,56	Jo's Forrest 36
Hockers Ridge 61	Indian Town 17	Jonathans Lot 64
* out of order		* James Meadows 54,58

Jonathans Meadow 94	Little Rock 78	McLellings Adventure 46
Jones Discovery 92	Limmerick 37,40	McQueens Choice 91
Jones' Lot 66	Lingons Neck 39	Majors Choice 85
Jones Farm 45	Litchfield City 61	Manheim Town 89
Josephs Favor 60	Little Brittain 81	Manor 27
Josephs Forest 60	Little More 19	Manors Privilege 5
Joshua's Gift 16	Little Muth 61	Mantion 51
Joshuas Lot 51,93	Little Proffit 89	Marshalls Desire 13,14,18
Judaths Delight 27	Littleworth 3	Marshalls Folly 79
Kelly's Delight 55	Littocks Folly 80	Martins Lot 64
Kidds Wilderness 77	Locks Lott 67	Martinton 51
Kildare 19	Loftins Lott 66	Mary's Adventure 39
Kindness Resurveyed 85	Logstons Addition 46	Mary's Delight 80,82
Kings Adventure 50	Long Crandon In the Hill 50,60	Mary's Meadows 56,58
Kings Evil 55	Long Hill 75	Mashes Mistake 60
Kingsbury Resurveyed 5	Long Island 59	Mashs Rest 84
Kirby's Range 76	Long Look 58	Matthews Forrest 14,53,79
Kitingers Glade 77	Long Point 2,42	Matthews Invention 78
Kitingers Orchard 77	Long Slipe 77	Matthews Meadows 53
Klinks Addition 90	Long Track 58	Mattocks Folly 17
Klinks Stoney Meadows 90	Long Trusted 19	Maxwells Habitation 85
Knavery Detected 44	Long Valley 49	Maynors Chance 67
Laburinth 44	Long Upland 38	Meadow 59
Labysmith 39	Long Valleys 58	Meadows Green 89
Lancaster 52	Longs Addition 7	Meadows Lott 67
Land of Promise 26,28,29, 31,32,36,93	Longs Dale 52	Meeleys Delight 95
	Longs Discovery 61	Melinda 50
Lanes Addition 88	Longsworth 1	Merediths Lot 68,69
Last Choice 19	Lott #22 -42	Merediths 2nd Lot 69
Lasting Pleasure 95	Louderslagers Meadows 92	Merrymans Addition 85
Lawsons Chance 34	Love & Unity 64	Merrymans Adventure 60
Lawsons Farm 28	Lovealis Addition 91	Merrymans Choice 74
Lawsons Project 69	Low Land 55	Merrymans Delight 56,57
Lawsons Range 67	Lowry's Lott 16	Merrymans Desire 78
Leaf Land 52	Ludwicks Berry 94	Merrymans Lot 84,85
Leafe 55	Lukes Adventure 40,41,42,38	Merrymans Mount 57
Lease 76	Lucky Addition 29	Merrymans Neck 78
lease land 29	Lukes Goodwill 7	Merrymans Neighbors 45
Leaves Chance 32	Lunns Lott 45	Merrymans Pasture 85
Lemmons Choice 56	Luthers Delight 92	Michaels Beginning 80
Lemmons Enlargement 54	Lynchs Desire 33	Michaels Chance 42
Lemmons Lot 55	Lyons Den 56	Middle Ridge 49
Lemmons Outlet 56	McComiskeys Habitation 79	Middle Rock 78
Lemmons Patch 56	McCubbins Addition 85	Milford Enlarged 19
Letter Loney 45	McGills Choice 89	Mill Place 17
Lightfoot 66	McLanes Venture 18	Millers Gain 92
Little Britain 75	McLanes Hills 18	Millers Gift 69
*Merrymans Beginnings 78		* Milford Haven 45,47
* out of order		

Millers Island 6
Millers Meadows 79
Milover 75
Modena 19
Modicum 94
Mollys & Sallys Delight 58
Mollys Garden 1
Mollys Industry 57
Monk's Discovery 47
Mordecais Folly 74
Mordecais Square 74
More or Less Certificate 52
Morgans Delight 49,85,87
Morgans Tent Reserveyed 13,15
Morning Choice 95
Morrises Lot 85
Morrows Venture 89
Mothers Friendship 89
Mount Hase 4,5,
Mount Joy 66
Mount Misery 74
Mount Pisga 16
Mount Pleasant 75,92
Mount Royal 84
Mountain 51
Mountain Town 94
Mulberry Point 37
Murrays Chance 78
Murrays Favor 93
Murrays Grotto 78
Murrays Plains 53,61
My Ladys Manor 29,36,65,69
Myers Wires 67
Mysers Care 52
Nancys Fancy 91
Nanjemy 30
Narrow Ridge 91
Naves Inspection 41
Neds & Wills Valleys & Hills 44
Neglect 76
Neighbours Friendship 19
New Found Bottom 96
New Germany 72,82,88
New Hills & Dales 78
New Land Mark 80

New Market 94
New Switzerland 88
New Tavern 17
New Town 94
Newks Hill 16
Newton 44
Nicholas Manor 49
Nicholsons Delight 44
Nicholsons Discovery 37,40 42
Nicholsons Manor 51,53,55, 56,57,76,77,90,93
Nicholsons Monument 76
Nights Addition 52
Nightstone 75
Noons Delight 80
Noons Pleasant Meadows 80
Norfolk 52
Norris' Addition 68
Norris' Adventure 68
Norris' Chance 66
Norris' Enlargement 68
Norris' Neighbor 68
Norris' Wonder 67
North & Southampton 58
North Canton 88,89
North Carolina 44,46,47
Northampton 55
Norwich 2,4
Nothing Worth 42
Nottingham 41
Nottings Lot 79
Novascotia(Nova Scotia 80,94
Ohio 74
Oblong 38
Olivers Lot 52,56,60
Organs Forest 47
Osbornes Lot 93
Others Neglect 61
Outlet to Bushey Neck 1
Overprone 79,95
Owners Landing 28,31
Oystons Choice 85
Painters Level 74
Pallentine 96
Panthers Hills 74

Panthers Level 54,77
Panthers Lodge 73
Paper Mills 77
Parade 94
Paradise 87
Paradise Regained 1,7
Parishes Fear 44,45
Parishes Neglect 7
Parkes Death 50
Parks Death Knott 57
Parletts Fancy 5
Parris(Parresh, Parrishes) Range 44,45,46,47,48
Parrishes Lott 76
Patent 68
Pavement 56
Pay My Debts 47
Peace & Good Neighbor 44
Peach Brandy 17
Peach Brandy Forrest 16,19
Pearces Defeat 74
Pearces Folly 56
Pearces Lot 57
Pearces Security 57
Pearrys (Pearys) Range 86,87
Peggy's Chance 17
Peggy's Delight 73
Penelope Dye & Thos. Cockey Dye's Addition 52
Perdues Lot 65
Perseverance 19
Peters Addition 76
Peters Leavings 19
Petersburgh 75,76
Petticoats Lodge 95
Petticoats Loose 92
Petty Spring 94
Philemons Lot 4
Philipsburgh 90
Piersons & Benj. Beginning 73
Pimlico 32,44
Pindalls Search 58
Piney Grove 69
Piney Hills 80
Piney Meadows 92
Pinsent Will 94
Pitt 80

*Pleasant Hills 80
Planton 94
Pleasant Garden 89,96
Pleasant Green 46
Pleasant Grove 88
Pleasant Meadows 73,78,91
Pleasant Valley 92
Pleasants Prospect 54,74
Ploughmans 65
Plowmans Fancy 94
Plowmans Park 92,94
Plumb Tree Bottom 15
Plunketts Lot 66
Plymouth 78
Pococks Lot 69
Point Espril 17
Point Esprite 17
Point Look Out 92
Point Pleasant 73
Pollygon 75
Pomerania 81
Poor Jamaica Mans Plague 50,51,59
Poor Mans Barrack 73
Poplar Neck 86
Pork Forest 26
Potters Lot 91
Pottsburgh 92
Pouths Gains 17
Poverty Parts Good Co'y. 56
Powells Desire 72
Powells Discovery 75,76
Powells Point 83
Presbureys Discovery 42
Prices Chance 58,81
Prices Delight 56,58
Prices Enlargement 58
Prices Favor 53
Prices Good Luck 58
Prices Good Will 51,55
Prices Hunting Ground 79
Prices Kindness 61
Prices Lott 69
Prices Outlet 58
Prium 81
Privilege 3,4,40
Project 2
Prospect 50,76
Providence 46
* out of order

Prusia 81
Purchase 66
Quarry 44
Quartermans Chance 73
Quartermans Choice 78
Quebecs Addition 46
Quinn 27
Rachels Prospect 56,61
Randalls Fancy 44
Ranging Forest 37
Rattlesnake Hill 94
Ravens Outlet 37
Reaves Neck 26
Red Oak Ridge 57
Reeds 64
Reeses Trial 94
Regulating (Regulated) Vineyard 52,75
Regulation 49,59
Reisters Study 1
Reserve 26,30
Ribbles Meadow 92
Rich Meadow 16,17,18
Rich Meadows 17
Richards Chance 93
Richards Conclusion 94
Richards Disappointment 17
Richards Hope 32
Richards Rectitude 94
Richardson 67
Richardsons Forest 3,4,5,
Richardsons Level 37
Richardsons Lot 65
Richardson Meadows 65
Richardsons Neglect 29
Richardsons Plains 41
Richardsons Prospect 39
Ridgely's Delight 47
Ridgelys Fancy 56
Rights Forest 41
Ristons Folly 80
Roberts Forest 56
Robinsons & James Delight 73,78,81
Rochester 13,14,16,18,19, 20,91,92,95,96,97
Rock Meadow 90
Rockholds Folly 69

*Ribbles Folly 88
Rockholds Lot 69
Rocky Point 4
Rogers Enlargement 44
Rogers Range 45
Roloss Adventure 26
Rome 78
Rope Walk 95
Rosemonds Fancy 41
Rotterdam 94
Round About Flat Top 81
Round About Neighbors 52
Rubys Lot 68
Rum 79
Rustehoof 96
Rutledges Delight 37
Rutters Folly 86
Ruxtons Range 83
St. Georges 42
St. Joseph's Privilege 42
Salisbury Plains 45,47,83
Sallys Lot 64
Sallys & Mollys Delight 53
Salt Petre Neck 37
Sams Meadow 46
Sampsons 67
Sampsons Folly 79
Samsons Farm 85
Samuels Addition 51
Samuels Hope 49
Samuels Lot 83
Samuels Meadows 51,58
Samuels Purchase 73
Sandy Bottom 13,15
Saplin (Sapling)Ridge 67,88
Saters Addition 58,59
Scheming Defeated 18,77
School Lot 17
Scotts Improvement 37
Seaport 96
Sea Ticks Plenty 83
Selsed 50
Severn Refuse 50
Sewells Fancy 30
Sewell Park 14
Shades 94
Shadricks Last Shift 15
Sharps Lot 69
Shawn Hunting Ground 50,51
(Shawan) 52,57,58

Shaws Delight 4	Sophias Garden Resurveyed 39	Stuckett 80
Shaws Fancy 4	Sparks Desire 67	Stumbling Block 5
Shaws Priviledge 4	Spicers Deer Park 76	Stumps Lott 82
Shenough 90	Spicers Stony Hills 47	Stute 30
Shepperds Lott 69	Spicers Inheritance 47	Suel (Sewell) 30
Shepherds Range 67,69	Sportsmans Hall 74,76,85,93	Sulset Othen 55
Sheredines Addition 56	Spot 64	Sulsett 58
Sheredines Bottom 4,5	Spring Garden 50,52,81,96	Susannah & Mary 54
Sheredines Meadow 56	Spring Hills 72	Surveyers Discovery 18
Sheredines Search 58	Spring Lott 73,74	Surveyors Point 41
Shillings Folly 77	Spring Run 81	Sute 26
Shillings Meadows 82	Springfield 77,78	Sutter Hill 59
Shillings Pleasure 81	Srusbury 1	Swallow Fork 37
Shipleys Choice 13	Stains Neglect 92	Swanson 29
Shitleys Lane 89	Standifords Chance 32	Sweeds Folly 45
Shitovers Choice 73	Standifords Lot 65	Talbots Forest 58
Shoemakers Hall 4	Stansburys Good Luck 59	Talbotts Lot 81
Shraders Desire 92	Stansburys Grove 75,77,79,81	Talbots Slavery 54,60
Shroads Range 96	Stansburys Inheritance 1,5,6,7	Taylors Addition 7
Shrusbery 76	Stansbury's Plains 50,56	Taylors Discovery 52,55
Sidling Hill 17	Stansuburys Vedsmight 6	Taylors Direction 52
Sidmons Last 3	Stephens Chance 73	Taylors Hall 52
Simms Chance 29	Stephens Hope 96	Taylors Inlargement 42
Simms Discovery 59	Stepney Crossway 18	Taylors Mount 42
Sinclairs Chase 67	Stevens Addition 81	Taylors Purchase 67,68
Singerys Chance 80	Stevens Folly 19,81	Taylors Pur'tis 28
Singerys Trouting Streams 80	Stevensons Hurtleberry Hills 80	Taylors String 49,54
Sings Range 61	Stevensons Manor 16,17	Teags Pleasant Ridge 56,59
S__less Dry Mountain 69	Stinchcombs Reserve 13	Teags Plenty Ridge 52
Small Hope 67,80	Stocksdales Grove 18	Teagues Ramble 13
Small Valley 39,41	Stocksdales Provision 18	Tetrix Folly 94
Small Valley Near 1	Stoffields Delight 91	Thomas' Choice 51,90,91
Small's Delight 94	Stones Adventure 49	Thomas' Frolick 68
Smallwood 54	Stoney Bottom 80	Thomas & John Cockeys
Smithfield 82	Stoney Crossway 16	Meadows 52
Smiths Addition 55	Stoney Hills 1,5,81,96	Thomas' Poor Spot 74
Smiths Chance 5	Stoney Hollow 73,75	Thomas' Purchase Resurvey
Smiths Fancy 19	Stoney Level 75	40
Smiths Lot 64	Stoney Point 6	Thomas' Range 85
Smiths Spring 96	*Stones Range 84	Thomas' Wentland 60
Snakes Den 65,88	Stoney Meadows 94	Thompsons Chance 30
S'o Addition 36	Stoney Ridge 76,83	Thompsons Choice 30,33,
Sollers Point 2	Stoney Spring 79	34
Sopetices Town 58	Stoney Ups & Downs 74	Thompsons Lot 38
Sophias Garden 2,4	Stoney Valley 95	Three Brothers 73,76
Sophiers Garden Regulated	Strawberry Patch 16,17	Tibs United Inheritance 40
(Sophias) 1,2,4,5,6,7	Strife 7,59	Timber Bottom 18
* out of order	* Thomas' Adventure 85	* Thomas' Folly 14

Timber Neck 14
Timber Ridge 47
Timber Swamp 6
Tipperary 90, 97
(Tipperara)
Tiptons 67
Tiptons Addition 61
Tiptons Puzzle 52, 60
Tivis Chance 19
Todds Delight 85
Todd's Forecast 54
Todds Forest 51
Todd (Todds) Range 46, 47, 86
Tolers Disappointment 2
Tom's Choice 44, 46, 47
Tower Hill 42
Towsons Chance 29
Towsons Grove 75
Towsons Inheritance 61
Traceys Hazard 81
Traceys Park 54
Transylvania 94, 96
Traymore 48
Triangle Neck 38, 40, 41
Tripple Union 86
Troy 80, 81
Truemans Acquaintance 28, 31
Tryangle 56
Two Bridges 72
Tullys Addition 61
Tully's Beginnings 61
Turkey Cock Hall 45, 93
Turkey Point 78
Turks Range 15
Turners Hll 46
Twins Purchase 13
Two Brothers 69
Ulricks Delight 75
Union 57
United Friendship 97
Upper Hagreton 95
Upper Marlborough 15, 16, 19
Valiant Hazard 47
Vaughans Inclosure 81
Vaughans Level 92
Vaughans Parade 81

Venters Adventure 39, 42
Venture Not 53
Violin 37
Volcania 49
Vulcane 60
Wages Trust 13, 14, 15, 18
Wallet 76
Warbore Hills 18
Wasons Farm 52
Water Oak Level 88
Water Oak Ridge 52
Watkins Desire 74
Watertons Neglect 28
Watson Trust 13, 14, 18, 19
Wedge 2
Wee Bitt (Bit) 88, 93, 94
Welches Cradle 57, 61
Wells Care 88, 90, 91
Welshes Discovery 14
Welshmens Venture 46
Wests Lot 92
Wheelers Chance 54, 61
Wheelers Enlargement 82
Wheelers Lot 82
Wheelers Purchase 82
Whiskey Bottle 72
White Hall 58, 59
White Oak Bottom 14, 17, 88
White Oak Swamp 2
White Rocks 72
Who Tho't It 27
Wibett 28
Widows Lot 68
Wifes Mill 95
Wignals Defence 28
William Refused 95
Wm. The Conqueror 29
Wm's. Addition 85, 95
Wm's. Beginning 60
Wm's. Chance Leased 49
Wm's. Defence 14
Wm's. Folly 55
Wm's. Forest 60
Wm's. Intent 13
Wm's. Lot 69

Wm's. Puzzle 60
Wm's. Refuge 29
Wm's. Struggle 80
Wilmots Grange 52
Wilmotts Meadows 15, 20
(Willmotts)
Willmots Retirement 76
Wilmotts Wells 61
Willmotts Mountain 13, 20
Willmots Wilderness 20
Wilsons Adventure 36
Wilsons Discovery 36
Wilsons Outlet 36
Wilsons Range 19
Winchesters Lot 89, 93, 96
Windles Rest 37
Winifreds Garden 33
Winsaw 95
Winsor 30
Winsor Forrest 14
Wisners Prospect 81
Wispau 75
Woodhome 90
Wooleys Range 44
Worthingtons Bottom 61
Wrights Range 90
Young Jacobs Chance 52
Young Mans Adventure 51
Young Mans Delight 76
Young Richards 50
Young's Delight 47
Youngs Escape 30, 32
Youngs Neglect 49

SURNAME INDEX

Abierism 37
Abraham 63
Adams 8,21,26,88
Adlesperer 72
Agan 62
Aikle 21
Ailer 88
Alceroad 72
Alexander 26,37
Aler 88
Alford 8
Algier 88
All 37
Allen 8,26,48,63
Allender 26,37
Allison 10,48
Alls 43
Allwood 62
Almack 72
Almoney 64
Alterfrit 87
Ambers 48
Ambrose 88
Amey 13
Amos 26
Amoss 49
Anderson 13,21,26, 49,64
Andrew 37
Andrews 37,49
Annells 21
Annis 8
Ansell 64
Anson 49
Apple 8
Arion 72
Armagust 72
Armitage 82
Armstrong 1,8,44, 63,64,82
Arnold 8,13,20,37 62,72,82
Asboury 20
Asher 1,37

Ashman 49,88
Ashpaw 21
Askew 8
Asque 26,35
Asquith 8
Aster 44
Aston 13
Ayres 64
Bachedlor 20
Bacon 64
Baddock 48
Bagford 49
Baggs 26
Bailer 8
Bailey 13,21,26,72, 73,89
Bain 26,35
Bailys 21
Baker 8,12,13,26, 27,30,35,48,64, 72,73,89
Baldwin 27
Ball 73
Ballard 8
Baltimore 44,83
Banfill 27
Barber 21,62
Bardell 14
Bared 62
Bareham 73
Berger 44
Barks 63
Barlow 21
Barnes 13,27
Barnett 44
Barney 21,22,44, 48,73
Barns 62
Barret 72
Barrey 12
Barrow 27
Barry 8
Barton 1,27,37
Bast 8

Bateman 38
Bates 13
Batty 83
Baughman 44
Baxley 44,48
Baxter 21,64,82,88
Bayhon 12
Baylis 1
Beach 8,13
Beam 44,48
Beard 8
Beasman 13
Beaver 13,20,21, 23,73
Beck 88
Beckley 89
Bell 14,43,44,88
Belleson 62
Belt 49,88,89
Benjamin 87
Benner 27
Bennett 13,14,20, 21,43,48
Bentle 8
Bentley 88
Bernard 21
Berry 8,37,43,48, 97
Beston 49
Beven 21
Bias 21
Bidderson 1
Biddle 1
Binnex 49
Bishop 27,62
Bivens 1,43
Blackrote 21
Blaze 89
Blatchley 49
Blizzard 88
Bloomer 44
Blueford 44
Blush 8
Boaring 62

Boes 73
Bole 21
Boles 37
Bolton 8
Bomgardner 88
Bond, 1,8,21,37,38, 44,49,64,72,82,88, 89
Boon 8
Boone 44
Bonner 62
Bonney 88
Boring 13,20,72,73
Bosley 27,49,63,64, 72,73
Bosman 64,72
Boss 21,25
Bossom 72
Boswell 1
Bott 8
Botts 13
Boucher 27
Bowen 27,49,62,72, 82,83
Bower 89
Bowers 8,14,44
Bowley 8,21,38,44
Boxley 48
Boyce 27,49
Boyd 21,50
Boyer 8
Brada 64
Bradfield 50
Bradley 8,21,27
Bradshaw 8,12
Bramley 27
Brangen 62
Brannan 37
Brasher 13
Bray 48
Bredenbough 8
Brees 27
Brereton 8
Brerton 27

Briley 38	Bush 8,89	Chance 28	Conway 21
Brimingham 21	Busling 44	Chandler 28	Cook 13,14,20,28
Britt 21	Bussey 27,35,72	Chapman 14,74	Cookson 51
Brittain 88	Butler 28,45,88,89	Chapple 21	Cooper 21,51,62,89
Britto 8	Button 21,48,72,82	Chase 1,38	Copes 21
Britton 27,38,43,73	Calder 74	Chattle 28	Corberth 48
Brock 83	Caldwell 62	Chears 28	Corbey 43
Brodbent 48	Caley 28	Chenowith 50,62	Corbin 8,28,51,62,
Brookman 21	Calgoe 21	Cherry 28	63,89
Brooks 13,21,44,50,72	Calhoun 21	Chilcoat 50,73	Cord 28
Brothers 13,20	Caltriter 74,75	Chilcote 12	Corderay 62
Brown 1,8,12,21,27,	Cambell 20	Childs 83	Corman 21
37,62,72,88,89	Cameron 21	Chine 38	Cornthwait 12
Brownattan 22	Camp 28	Chinnowith 14	Corthwaite 45
Bruce 89	Campbell 74	Chitham 62	Corrithwait 21
Brumagen 63	Canady 48	Christopher 1	Corrothers 21
Brumpft 87	Cannady 28	Clark 2,8,20,21,50	Corwin 21
Bruthenton 27	Caple 73	Clarke 2,28,43,45	Coteney 38
Bryan 8,13,37,82	Carback 1,38	Clawey 50	Cottman 62
Bryant 21,50	Carey 12,62	Claws 63	Cottrill 2,38
Bryson 8	Carlinger 75	Clay 8,28	Councilman 2
Bublets 79	Carlyle 21	Clayton 28	Cousins 28
Buchanan 1,8,14,21,	Carman 65	Clemmons 21	Coutz 75
27,44,48,50,83	Carnan 28,50	Cline 43	Covenhover 28
Buck 1,8,27,37,38,	Carr 73	Clouse 74	Cow 2,8,63
64	Carrol 38	Coale 2	Cowan 38
Buckingham 13,20,	Carroll 21,45,50	Cockey 45,50,51	Cowell 45,48
44,48	Carrs 14	Cockland 21	Cowerd 2
Bufort 8	Carson 21	Coddo 51	Cowing 28
Bull 8,64,72,73	Carter 1,7,12,28,	Coe 62	Cox 2,28,51,65,74,83
Burches 43	83	Cole 2,20,21,38,51	Cradock 51
Burgess 27,62	Cartright 38	62,73,74,75,83,87	Cragg 45
Burgin 1	Case 87	Colegate 51,83	Craig 8
Burk 50,64,65	Casey 8,89	Colinas 28	Craighead 21
Burkett 21	Casley 62	Collett 74	Crammit 89
Burkhead 62	Casloe 75	Collins 8,21,25,43	Crampton 21
Burling 83	Cassady 45	Colter 21	Crawford 45,48
Burm 87	Catere 75	Colvin 38	Crawner 28
Burn 8,87	Cathart 87	Collogan 8	Craymer 20
Burner 21	Cathcart 28	Combs 28,35	Crayoner 14
Burnett 62	Catore 89	Connaway 14	Creagh 89
Burnham 50,62	Cats 73	Conneley 89	Creter 89
Burns 21,65,88,89	Caum 87	Connely 89	Crips 21
Burtle 8	Cavenden 65	Conner 14,21	Crisswell 14,20
Burton 27	Chamberlain 28	Connor 21	Cristerson 63,65
Busbey 72	Chambers 21,43	Connoway 38	Cristoson 51
Busby 72	Chamier 83	Constable 12	Crockett 21

-109-

Crohorn 75
Croker 8
Cromwell 2,28,29,
　33,45,51
Crook 38
Crosbley 48
Croskey 28
Cross 14,74,75,83
Crotinger 75
Crouder 89
Crowder 45,83,91
Croxall 43
Crudgengton 28
Crumrine 75
Crumwell 38
Cullam 29
Cullins 74
Cullison 62,73,74
Cummins 74
Cunningham 12,63,
　65,83
Curgan 12
Curl 38
Currier 65
Curtin 21
Curtis 65
Curtiss 63
Daley 65
Dallis (Dollis)2
Darnel 34
Darnell 29
Darr 48
Daughaday 52
Daugherday 2
Davey 12,22
Davidson 12,22,24
Davis 2,15,20,21
　22,39,75,83,89
Davison 65
Davy 52
Dawson 21,22,24
Day 62,89
Deal 83
Deale 90
Deames 45
Dean 29,38,89
Dear 29

Deaver 15,62,83
Decker 89
Deeds 75
Defnist 48
Delaney 39
Delaport 22
Deshield 22
Dew 2
Diat 12
Dick 15
Dickinson 22
Dilling 15
Dillon 65
Dimien 43
Dimmitt 29,45,65
Dimmonck 65
Ditto 29,35
Divers 29
Dixon 52,65
Dizard 87
Dobbin 29
Dodd 52
Dollenton 63
Donnalson83
Donnell 22
Donnevan 29
Donton 39
Dorsey 14,15,22,29,
　39,75
Dorson 89
Dougherty 21,22
Doughty 29
Downey 75
Downing 2
Downs 29
Doyl 22,75
Doyle 87,89
Drewit 62
Duckart 48,90
Due 29
Duff 8
Duffill 75
Duhurst 83
Dukes 2
Dulaney 52
Dulany 29
Duly 29

Dun 62
Dungan 45
Dunham 75
Dunkin 75
Dunqin 39
Dye 52
Eady 29,32
Eaglestone 2,83
Earmin 29
Eason 62
Edward 43
Edwards 15,52,62,65,
　75,83
Elder 15,39
Electan 22
Ellicott 12
Ellinor 52
Elliott 22,29,63,65
Embler 75
Enders 45
Englan 62
Enloes 29,65
Ensor 12,22,45,52,
　62,65,75,83,89,90
Epaugh 90
Errickson 22
Erwin 29
Evans 15,22,29,83
Everhart 90
Everitt 29
Ervin 43
Fair 76
Fannett 62
Farrill 52
Farver 15,20
Fauble 76,90
Feather 76
Fell 22,39,62
Feller 22
Felton 39,62
Fenwick 65
Ferrill 62
Ferrow 87
Fetterly 90
Field 29
Fielding 30
Fields 63

Fife 2
Fights 75
Fin 87
Finder 75
Finlay 15
Finley 90
Fisher 15,76,90
Fishpaugh 53
Fitch 2
Fite 45
Fitzgerald 11
Fitzhugh 30,33,34
Fitzmorris 30
Flairs 43
Flanagan 29,30
Flatt 62
Flaugherty 22
Flax 22
Floyd 3
Forbes 22
Ford 8,12,30,48,53,
　65,75,76
Foreman 76,90
Forney 90
Fort 53
Foster 22,30,53,65
Fouble 90
Foulger 22
Fowler 3,15,30,39
Fox 30,63
Foye 22
France 12
Frances 53
French 39,90
Frankford 90
Franklin 3,15,30,36,
　45,62,76
Franks 90
Frazier 76,90
Freeland 65
Freeman 63
French 22,43
Fresh 76
Frissell 15
Frog 90
Frost 30
Fryfogle 90

Fugate 65	Goodwin 15,22,30,	Hackley 31	Hellems 23
Fuller 43,65	34,62,63,65,66	Haden 16	Hellin 22
Fus 12	Gordon 22,30,63	Hadley 87	Helms 45,92
Gad 30	Gore 53,62,90	Haff 22	Henderson 22
Gaine 76	Gorman 22	Haghn 91	Hendley 66
Gall 76	Gorsuch 15,29,30,	Hail-Haile 12,45,66,	Hendon 31
Gallaway 30,39	53,62,63,66,83,	84	Hendrickson 39,40,43
Galloway 3,53,65	84,91	Hair 77	Heney 91
Gardner 30,45,48	Gosnell 20	Hale 3,10,54,62,77	Hennick 45
Garlets 76	Gossick 39,43	Hall 12,22,31,45,	Hensman 22
Garns 22	Gott 30,54,62	54,63	Herbert 62
Garrettson 3	Gottier 22	Hallcok 77	Hesam 22
Garrison 22	Gough 15,39,43	Hamilton 10,22	Hess 4,91
Garritson 39	Govane 54,84	Hammond 10,22,54,91	Hewit 15,16,20,62,63
Garts 22	Graham 15	Hampton 39	Hickman 4
Gash 83	Grammer 91	Hanager 31	Hicks 55,63,66,77,92
Gatch 3,8	Grant 3	Handon 39	Higginbottom 22
Gather 22	Graves 3	Hanes 15	Hill 32,54
Gaughn 15	Gray 43,84	Hannah 22	Hillen 4,10
Gent 53,76	Green 3,12,22,30,	Hannakay 91	Hillenger 4
Gerritt 45	39,43,54,62,63,	Hanson 10,40,45,48,	Hilton 32,35,36
Gettier 24	66,76,83,87,91	84	Hims 39
Gest 3	Greenfield 31	Harbour 43	Hines 32
Gibbons 3,22	Greenland 91	Harden 76	Hinsom 22
Gibbs 65	Grigory 3	Hardley 87	Hions 91
Gilbert 63,65	Griffen 39	Hare 77	Hirast 87
Gilberthrop 53	Griffeth 12,22,39	Harper 22,63	Hiser 84
Giles 84	Griffin 31,43	Harrimon 39,43,54	Hitton 28
Gill 53,76,90,91	Griffith 3,12,15,31,	Harris 48,91	Hoffman 10,66
Gillesland 53	45,54,62,84,87	Harrison 10,31,84	Hoofman 77
Gillingham 65	Grimes 3,22,39,83	Harritt 27,31	Hoggers 63
Gillis 65	Grist 22	Harryman 3,4,6,63,87	Holbrooks 4
Gist 53,76,84,91	Grogg 76	Hart 40,54,84	Hollbrooks 40
Gittings 22,30,34,36	Gross 91	Hartley 31	Holems 24
Given 65	Grove 3	Hartman 10,12,77	Holland 32
Gladman 15	Grover 31,39,43,66	Harvey 55,63	Holliday 55,92
Glen 87	Gudgeon 30,31,36	Harwood 62	Hollin 39
Glynn 22	Guin 31	Hassey 12	Hollingsworth 10,22
Goare 62	Guiten 28	Hatherington 62	Holmes 22,87,91
Goddard 65	Guiton 31,34,35	Hatton 31,39	Holston 10
Godman 22	Gullivan 63	Haun 91	Holton 89,91
Golding 30	Gumins 63	Hawkins 16,20,23,43,	Hon 12
Goldsmith 30	Gunkell 91	77	Honan 22
Goodchild 62	Gurnel 22	Hayes 16,22,66,91	Honley 10
Goodfellow 76	Guthery 22,31	Haywood 10	Hoofman 74
Goodhall 62	Gwin 34	Headington 12,31,54	Hook 10,16,44,45
Goodman 62	Hackett 10	Heatherington 10	Hooke 16

Hooker 16,54,92	Jaffres 48	Keneday 10	Legge 23,40
Hooper 32,48	James 23,32,62,	Kennedy 77	Legget 40
Hopham 22	63,92	Kerkehiser 77	Leggitt 87
Hopkins 22,32,55,63, 84	Jamison 4,32	Ketchpot 55	Legue 43
	Jarrett 10	Kelso 10	Lemmon 10,23,55,56, 63,78
Hornby 10,12	Jarman 4	Keysted 23	
Horner 10	Jarvis 45	Kidd 32,77	Leonard 48
Horrick 77	Jeer 10	Killinger 10	Letzinger 10
Horton 16	Jeffereys 10	Kimbo 23	Lewis 46,63,67
Hosiel 77	Jenkins 32	King 4,55,92	Levi 10
Houck 91	Jennings 40	Kingsbridge 23	Lindenberger 10
Houk 91	Jerman 43	Kittinger 77	Lindsay 16,23,24
House 84	Jermin 40,43	Kittleman 84	Link 62
Housely 63	Jermon 43	Kneff 16,20	Lippo 92
Howard 16,32,34,40 45,84,87,91	Jervis 16	Knewoom 16	Liscomb 10
	Job 23	Knight 45,55	Liston 10
Hubbard 48	Johns 23	Kramer 46,48	Littear 92
Hudson 4,5,15,16,92	Johnson 4,10,23, 24,32,45,46, 55,62,63,66, 77,87	Labold 23	Littig 12,23
Huff 16		Lacey 63	Litzinger 10
Hughes 10,22,40,43, 63,66		Lackfingers 23	Lobeshess 67
		Lagett 32,33	Logan 23
Hunt 32,36,55,66	Johnston 23,63	Lamwert 78	Logsdon 17
Hunter 32,55,66	Jonas 63	Lane 10,16,62,84, 89,92	Logue 17
Hurst 77	Jones 4,10,16,23, 32,40,43,45, 55,62,63,66, 84,92		Loney 33
Husk 10		Langford 23	Long 4,10,16,22, 23,56,78
Husse 22		Langton 4	
Hussel 10		Lard 20	Longley 46
Hutchins 32,63,66	Jonus 62	Larie 23	Lonsell 16
Hutchinson 10	Jordan 10,12,16, 77	Larkin 23	Lorah 12
Hyle 20		Lattimore 33	Louderman 23
Hyner 22	Joseph 62	Laughlin 84	Louderslager 92
Hynim 63	Joy 92	Laurence 23,33,46 48	Love 10,16,46,56, 67,84
Hyott 62	Joyce 10,23,84		
Ingram 10	Kailer 77	Lavelly 23	Loveall 92
Inloes 23	Kalebough 77	Lavely 16	Lovedon 78
Ireland 4	Katohey 10	Lawder 40	Lucas 17,33,67
Irwin 23	Keefer 92	Lawrence 10,17,25 48,63	Ludley 33
Isgrig 32	Keener 23		Lusha 23
Isler 62	Kees 23	Lawson 46,67	Lux 16,17,40,46,56, 58,67,84,93
Isor 62	Keeth 77	Laypole 23	
Ivory 4	Keith 77	Leach 67,84	Lye 56
Jacks 16	Kell 23	Leaf 46	Lynch 33,40,56, 63,84
Jackson 4,8,10,12, 23,32	Keller 10,23	Leage 23	
	Kelley 89,92	Lecky 23	Lynox 4
Jacobs 10,16,20,23, 26	Kelly 16,23,55	Leddick 12	Lyon 46,56,93
	Kelsey 67	Lee 23,33,48,62	Lynch 10
Jaffery 23	Kennaday 62	Leeke 10	Lynderman 20

-112-

Lyston 4	Major 20	Miller 5,10,17,23,33,	Nailor 11
Lytle 63,67	Male 56,63	48,63,67,78,79,93	Nappett 48
McAlister 46	Mallone 56	Milliken 10	Nash 33,93
McAllister 17	Malone 33,78	Mince 78	Neal 34,85
McBoyle 67	Maloney 78	Miniken 48	Neel 11,24,33,34
McBride 23,62	Maltison 25	Minkey 79	Neighbours 48
McBridge 23	Manahan 10	Mins 48	Nelson 48
McBroom 33	Manis 40	Minshire 46	Nesil 87
McCabe 10	Manning 17	Minsky 23	Netherclift 93
McCandles 11	Mansfield 10	Miser 43	Nets 48
McCann 33,35	Markey 4,78,79	Mitchel 17,22,24	Newberry 34
McCarty 33,56	Marsh 10,12,33,	Mitchell 23	Newley 67
McCausland 23	78,93	Moale 5,10,12,57,85	Newton 34
McClaslin 33	Marshal 78,79	Mock 40	Nice 11
McClung 63,67	Marshall 11,67,79	Molsby 11	Nichols 34
McComiskey 79	Marshel 40	Monk 24	Nicholson 11,40,57,
McCreery 23	Martin 43,78	Moody 84	63,67
McCubbin 33,56	Marton 85	Moore 5,10,11,12,17,	Nitzer 5
McCullen 24	Mason 48,62	26,33,40,46,48,57,	Noon 11
Mc Dannell 33	Mather 23	78,93	Norman 62
McDonnell 10	Matthews 10,23,56,	More 23	Norris 57,63,67,68
McFadden 85	78,79,89,93	Morgan 23,33,46,78	Norwood 5,57,79,
McFaddon 10	Mattox 4	Morris 5,10,23,67	85,87
McFall 33	Maxwell 23	Morrison 23,46,48	Nox 11
McGaw 67	May 40,43,46	Mortar 79	Null 79
McGee 17	Mays 24	Morton 67	Numle 24
McGrill 33	Mayson 23	Morris 11	Oats 93
McGurie 23	Meads 40	Moss 23	O'Brien 34
McKean 24	Meale 10	Motherly 57	O Brient 24
McKeever 23,24	Medlicote 78	Muday 11	Offell 62
McKim 23	Meekener 63,67	Mulberry 5	Ogg 18,20
McKinley 85	Mehaney 40	Mull 11	Ogden 57
McLane 20	Meredith 63,67	Mullan 10,11	Ogle 34
McLaughlin 33	Mernam 78	Mullen 23	Oldham 67
McLelling 46	Merrham 62	Mullin 40	Olive 11
McLure 23	Merritt 5	Mumma 10	Oliver 40
McMachan 23,24	Merryman 5,10,11,	Mummer 5	Oniel 24
McPhersons 10	17,46,56,57,62,	Mummy 46	Onion 34
McSwaney 33	63,67,78,79,85,	Munch 93	Onnick 24
Maccubbin 85	93	Murray 11,23,24,40,	Oram 5
Mackelfresh 17	Messer 11	78,84,93	Orndorf 46,48
Mackey 11	Middleton 23	Murphy 20,84	Orme 46
Madden 62	Middy 23	Musgrove 97	Orr 93
Magness 33	Migley 62	Myers 10,11,24,33,	Orrick 57,79
Major 17	Miles 40,43	46,67,78,93	Osborne 93
Maidwell 84,85	Millaman 33	Nace 93	Osburn 24
Maise 56	Mildews 40	Nailer 57,79	Ouslar 18

Owen 24,57,79	Petty 5	Ramsey 24	Ritaker 47,87,94
Owens 11,41	Philips 11,20,34,48	Randal 80	Ritter 48
Owings 17,18,20,34, 57,79,93	Phillips 18,57	Randall 58,62	Roach 20,48
Oyston 85	Philpot 11,57	Randle 68	Roades 62
Page 87	Pickett 57	Raven 6,41	Roads 34
Paine 57	Pindall 58	Rawlings 80	Roberts 6,11,24, 34,43,80,94,97
Painter 85	Pierly 94	Rea 24,34,41	Rochester 62
Pan 24	Pine 24,43	Reader 47	Rock 41
Pannell 24	Pitts 58,79	Ready 85	Rockhart 62
Panon 24	Pixley 94	Reams 11	Rockhold 63,68,69
Parker 24,34,41,63, 68	Plant 63	Rease 85	Rodes 63
Parks 41,43,57	Plowman 91,94	Reaves 34,41	Rodgers 63
Parlett 5	Pluck 46,48	Rebout 6	Roe 11,24
Parrish 18,48,63,68, 73,79	Plumb 18	Redison 48	Rogers 24,34,41, 43,47,58,62,63, 80,85,87
Patridge 5,85	Pocock 68	Reed 11,34,41,47,68	
Patterson 5,11,68	Poe 79	Reese 11,94	
Pattman 18	Pollad 62	Reiley 47	Rollings 6
Pauley 11	Pool 11,68	Renner 41	Roney 28,34
Pawling 5	Popped 62	Renshaw 6	Roof 94
Peachy 94	Porketts 11	Rettenberg 11	Rooles 18
Peacock 20	Porter 5,24,34	Rhode 68	Roop 80,94
Pearce 34,41,57,63, 68,85	Ports 94	Rhodes 63,94	Rosenberry 34
	Possen 34	Ribble 94	Ross 11,24
Pearson 11	Potter 6	Rice 20,27,34,47,80	Rouse 24
Peckwood 5,43	Powell 58	Richards 6,94,95	Rowan 35
Peddicort 79	Powers 24	Richardson 34,63,68	Rowen 34
Peleg 11	Prath 24	Richart 94	Rowles 87
Pennington 5,57,85	Pratt 6,11	Richie 11	Rowland 58,84,87
Peormy 85	Presbury 41,43	Ricks 11	Rownam 62
Penrice 24	Press 24	Ricketss 24	Royston 69
Peper 12	Preston 48	Riddle 11,62	Rublets 79
Perdue 34,68	Prian 58	Ridecker 41	Ruby 69,80
Perego 79	Price 11,46,47,48, 58,62,68,79,94	Ridenger 63	Rummage 41
Peregoy 57		Rider 11	Runnells 11
Perigoy 57	Prine 68	Ridge 24	Rus 24
Perine 41,87	Pringle 24	Ridgely 6,11,18,31, 34,41,47,58,68, 80,85,86	Rush 6
Perkins 87	Proctor 43		Rusk 24,47
Perkipile 79	Prosser 58		Russ 24
Perrigoe 85	Puntany 46	Riely 11,12	Russell 11
Perry 34,48	Purviance 24	Rigby 33,34	Ruth 6
Person 87	Pycraft 62	Rigdon 47,48	Rutledge 24,43,47, 63,69
Peters 24,79	Pye 62	Right 24	
Petra 79	Qua 41	Rimmer 6	Rutter 47,48,86
Petticoat 94	Quarterman 68	Rine 24	Ryan 11,35,85
	Ragan 62	Rinehart 80,94	Ryston 69
	Rain 87	Rion 35	Rywood 62
	Rainbow 87	Risteau 58	
		Riston 80	

S_____ 25	Shaw 6,24,35,69,86	Slater 24,86	Stevenson 18,19,47, 59,62,63,81,86,96
Sadler 58	Shawl 80	Slaymaker 11,59	
Salbowker 95	Shaws 86	Slee 35	
Sampson 25,63,69	Shay 62	Slimmer 12	Steward 24
Sanders 6,25,29,35,41	Sheets 24	Sloan 35	Stewart 12,35,48,59
Sands 24	Shepard 63,69	Sly 11	Stifer 7
Sank 11	Shepherd 12,47	Smith 6,11,12,19,24, 25,26,28,35,47,48, 59,62,69,80,81,86, 95	Stigar 47
Sanks 35	Sherner 95		Stiger 81,95
Sap 81	Shids 47		Still 41,43
Sapp 95	Shieighley 25		Stiner 80
Sappington 35	Shields 25,86	Snaler 35	Stinchcomb 7
Sater 58,59	Shilling 11,12,80	Snap 95	Stinebaugh 80
Sauble 81	Shillingberg 25	Snider 12,95	Stites 62
Saul 43	Shipley 19,63,69	Sollars 59,62	Stocksdale 18
Savage 11	Shires 43	Sollers 25,86,95	Stoddard 24
Savory 24	Shock 11	Solman 24	Stoddart 80
Sawyer 62	Shoehorn 25	Sparks 63	Stoker 24
Say 28,35	Shoffer 25	Spear 12,25,35,42,86	Stone 35,59,62
Schaeffer 24	Shorter 63	Speares 25	Stonebrinckner 81
Scarf 35	Showers 95,96	Speck 11,12	Stoney 21
Scarffe 59	Shriek 12	Spencer 48	Storey 25,43,96
Schooles 18	Shrier 95	Spicer 6,35,47	Storm 95
Scorey 12	Shriver 97	Spindle 80	Stout 19
Scott 11,59	Shuster 95	Spittler 95	Stranbell 24
Seagersley 12	Shutter 35	Splitstones 63	Strawbridge 35
Seddon 41,42	Sibre 48	Spriggs 86	Strickland 59,95
Sedge 59	Sich 95	Sriver 35	Strider 11
Seigler 25	Sides 86	Staines 95	Stringer 18
Selby 19	Silvester 11	Stains 19	Strong 35
Sellars 95	Simcock 87	Standiford 35,63	Stubbin 80
Sellers 35	Simmons 59	Stansbury 6,7,11,24,25 35,41,59,63,80,81, 86,95,96	Stuart 11,42
Sellman 18,19,20,47	Simms 35,69		Sucker 43
Selman 18,69	Simon 35		Sullivan 11,42,80
Selvey 19	Simpson 12,25,87	Stansby 25	Sumbolt 11
Sense 95	Sims 6	Starrett 47	Summers 25
Sergent 87	Sinclair 25,42	Stchudy(see Tschudy)12	Sunderland 35
Serjeant 35	Sinclaire 24	Steal 20	Sutton 25,41,43,63
Service 25	Sindall 6,86	Stediford 59	Swan 35,48
Sewell 26	Sindell 6,7,86	Steel 25,87	Swaney 59
Sh___ue 25	Singrey 80	Steigar 11	Swarth 27,35
Shakespear 6	Sinkler 69	Stelce 80	Sweeting 86
Shangles 80	Sinnerd 69	Stembler 19	Swingle 47,48
Shareman 81	Skeppy 23	Sterling 12	Swords 97
Sharp 69	Skinner 42,43	Sterrett 25,87	Sykes 62
Sharpe 59,96	Skipper 80	Sterrip 95	Sylvia 11
Shaul 80	Slade 69	Stett 25	Talbot 60,63
Shaver 80,95	Slagle 95	Stevens 11,24,35,59,96	Talbott 19,20,59,86

-115-

Tanner 96	Tuckett 12	Wareham 82	Willis 12
Tatley 60	Tuder 36	Warfield 60	Willsin 25
Taylor 7,12,35,42,47,	Tudor 36,60,62	Warner 36	Williamson 7,25
48,60,86,87	Tugood 43	Warren 25,48	Willmot 20
Teanor 20	Tull 25	Warrington 6,7,43	Willmoth 7
Tennor 19	Tumbledown 12	Warwick 82	Willson 12,19,20,
Tevis 19	Tumblinson 25	Wasky 24,25	25,42,63,82
Theoble 35	Turner 25,60,86,96	Waters 25,43	Wilmot 97
Thomas 42,60,96	Turnpaugh 60	Watkin 82	Wilmott 60,61,62
Thompson 7,13,19,28,	-Tye 60	Watkins 36,43,87	Wilson 8,12,36,48
36,60,97	Tyler 25	Watson 63	Wily 82
Thornbery 12	Tyson 12,36	Watts 7,87	Winchester 97
Thorpe 96	Umphries 25	Weatherby 26	Wineman 26
Thrash 60	Underwood 96	Weaver 12,25,96,97	Wing 25
Tibbett 25,26,63	Uppercoe 96	Weatherteurn 25	Wingender 25
Tillyard 25	Urill 19	Webb 25	Winks 12,62,82
Tinfill 19	Usher 25	Webster 12,25	Winning 25
Tinker 25	Van Bibber 25,47	Weeb 87	Winslet 36
Tipton 19,60,81	Vanbibber 87	Welch 12,25,96	Winteringer 62
Tivis 19,20	Vanderson 25	Wells 12,19,20,25,	Wisner 81
Tobitt 48	Vandevote 25	26,36,87	Wispaw 12
Todd 7,25,36,47,86	Vann 60	Welsh 19,48	Witen 36
Tolley 42	Vaughan 81	Wentz 82	With 87
Tomer 96	Vaugh 96	Werry 25	Wolf 81
Tool 25	Vaughn 60,63	Wertenberg 12	Wollar 42
Toone 86	Vaun 12	Wertian 19	Wood 42
Toppin 7	Vennel 36	Wery 21	Woodard 87
Towson 47,48,60,62	Virble 47	West 12,25,87,97	Woodcock 12,81
Tracey 25,60,62,81	Voice 42	Westfield 36	Wooden 36,96
Trapnell 60	Wages 20	Westley 96	Woodford 82
Trapt 36	Waggoner 82	Weston 42	Woodhouse 48
Trash 19	Wagster 25	Wetherton 42	Wooding 48
Traverse 86	Wainor 12	Wheatley 25	Woods 25,61
Traves 12	Waistcoate 25	Wheeler 7,12,19,61,	Woodward 87
Travis 25,63	Walker 12,20,25,48,	62,81,82,87	Woolery 20
Treagle 12	60,62,82,87,96	White 7,25,35,36	Woolf 36,48,61,96
Tredwell 36	Wall 7,12	Whitely 36	Woolrick 87
Tremble 25	Wallage 7	Wicks 36	Worrell 62
Trimble 48,60	Valley 42	Widerfield 61	Worthing 97
Trinsham 7	Wallton 20	Wiggott 96	Worthington 12,26,
Tripolete 12	Walraft 60	Wigley 7,25,42	61,62
Trippier 12	Walsh 25	Wiles 63	Wright 36,42,48,61
Trotten 7,86	Walter 12,42	Wiley 63	Wybland 97
Troyer 96	Walton 42	Wilkinson 12,87	Wyman 82
Tschudy 24,47	Wannell 25	Willaby 25	Yane 61
(see Stchudy)	Wantland 60	Willeme 7	Yates 12
Tucker 12	Ward 12,25,42	Williams 2,12,20,24,	Yellott 26
		25,26,36	Yem 26

Yiever 12	Yoiser 26	Young 12,26,30,36,40	Zene 26
Yinglins 97	York 36	42,47,48,61,62,97	

Other Heritage Books by Robert W. Barnes
and Bettie Stirling Carothers

1783 Tax List of Baltimore County

Index of Baltimore County Wills, 1659–1850

Other Heritage Books by Robert W. Barnes:

Baltimore and Fell's Point Directory of 1796

Baltimore County, Marriage References, 1659–1746

Baltimore County, Maryland Deed Abstracts, 1659–1750

Gleanings from Maryland Newspapers, 1776–85

Gleanings from Maryland Newspapers, 1786–90

Gleanings from Maryland Newspapers, 1791–95

*Index to Marriages and Deaths in the
Baltimore County Advocate, 1850–1864*

Other Heritage Books by Bettie Stirling Carothers:

1776 Census of Maryland

*1783 Tax List of Maryland, Part I:
Cecil, Talbot, Harford and Calvert Counties*

Maryland Oaths of Fidelity

Maryland Source Records: Volume 1

www.ingramcontent.com/pod-product-compliance
Lightning Source LLC
Chambersburg PA
CBHW070453090426
42735CB00012B/2540